South-East Asian Social Science Monographs

Zapin

Zapin
Folk Dance of the Malay World
Mohd Anis Md Nor

SINGAPORE
OXFORD UNIVERSITY PRESS
OXFORD NEW YORK
1993

Oxford University Press, Walton Street, Oxford OX2 6DP
Oxford New York Toronto
Delhi Bombay Calcutta Madras Karachi
Kuala Lumpur Singapore Hong Kong Tokyo
Nairobi Dar es Salaam Cape Town
Melbourne Auckland Madrid
and associated companies in
Berlin Ibadan

Oxford is a trade mark of Oxford University Press

Published in the United States
by Oxford University Press, New York

© Oxford University Press Pte. Ltd., Singapore, 1993

British Library Cataloguing in Publication Data
Data available

Library of Congress Cataloging-in-Publication Data
Mohd., Anis Md. Nor, 1955–
Zapin, folk dance of the Malay world/Mohd. Anis Md. Nor.
p.   cm.
ISBN 0-19-588598-8
1. Zapin (Dance)—History.   I. Title.
GV1796.Z34M64   1993
793.3'19595—dc20
92-20381
CIP

Typeset by Typeset Gallery Sdn. Bhd., Malaysia
Printed in Singapore by Kyodo Printing Co. (S) Pte. Ltd.
Published by Oxford University Press Pte. Ltd.,
Unit 221, Ubi Avenue 4, Singapore 1440

To Ana

Preface

THE performance traditions of Malaysia have received much less scholarly attention than those of other countries in South-East Asia, such as Indonesia, Thailand, and the Philippines. This may be because of the general lack of interest in Malaysia in fields of inquiry which most of the local population consider have little or no bearing on the economic well-being of the people and country.

Young Malaysians acquire only limited knowledge of the performance traditions through the national school system and there are no public or private institutions for the study of indigenous performance traditions. Instead, young Malaysians learn other forms of performance traditions. Private music schools where one can learn to play the piano or the violin are relatively plentiful in cities and towns, whereas opportunities to learn and play traditional indigenous instruments such as the *rebab* (traditional fiddle) and *gamelan* (ensemble of gongs) in formal school settings do not exist. Similarly, in the field of dance, one can easily take ballet lessons in private ballet schools but it is nearly impossible to learn Malay traditional folk and classical dances. Classes in these dances are limited to the informal settings of cultural clubs and organizations that espouse the learning and performing of traditional genres as part of the groups' cultural activities. Young Malaysians often learn traditional indigenous performances by chance rather than by choice.

Although a handful of folk dance genres are taught in schools, they remain separate from the general school curriculum. Instead, these traditions are taught for the purpose of providing public entertainment at school sports events and during school concerts at the end of the year. In universities and colleges, the same phenomenon prevails. It was only in the 1970s that universities began offering courses in the study of traditional performance genres. However, the courses offered fulfil only a small part of the requirements for the degree of Bachelor of Arts, Humanities and Social Sciences.

The fact that many foreign scholars interested in the study of South-East Asian performance traditions have bypassed Malaysia and concentrated their research on Indonesia, Thailand, and the Philippines has deprived Malaysia of a Western scholarly perspective on the study of indigenous performance genres. With only a handful of local scholars attempting to fill this gap, dance and music in Malaysia await further exploration: there are still vast lacunae in the holistic study of Malaysian traditional performances.

It is hoped that this book will be able to reduce the imbalance between Malaysia and other South-East Asian countries in the study of dance and music. The main intention of this book is to provide insight into the evolution of the *zapin* dance in Malaysia, and, in so doing, to shed light on how the movement of the Malays to widely dispersed areas within the region of the Straits of Malacca has influenced the development of particular forms of the dance genre.

Zapin as a Malay Performing Art

Zapin has clearly played, and continues to play, a significant role in the Malay performing arts, and therefore offers a fascinating opportunity for the study of the origin and evolution of a major art form. The role of Malay cinematography from the late 1940s to the mid-1960s has been a crucial link between the archaic form (*Zapin Melayu*) and the contemporary form of *zapin*; today, the latter has become one of the four pan-Malaysian folk dance traditions. The evolution of a regional folk tradition into a mainstream national folk tradition over a period of four decades can be attributed to the role played by the Malay movie industry through its talented movie directors, music composers, and dance choreographers. The versatility of *zapin* in adapting to new ideas or deriving inspiration from other genres has been an important factor in the continuous flow of new dance motives into contemporary *zapin*. In the early 1960s, *zapin* culled inspiration for new choreography from Western and Latin dances, which were then very popular. The cha-cha-cha (commonly referred to as the cha-cha), the samba, and the mambo, to name a few, provided inspiration to the late P. Ramlee, a leading movie star–singer–musician–dancer. He composed new musical scores, improvised within the existing genres, and introduced new dance motives, while retaining the four-beat element of the *zapin* dance phrase. In the 1970s, fancy footwork and hand movements, as well as the improvised movements of the head and torso, were the norm.

The complexity in performance style resulting from the increasing number of dance motives and fancier footwork has turned *zapin* into a dance which requires rehearsals before performances. In other words, contemporary *zapin* has become more rigid and structured than village *zapin*. It is performed on the proscenium stage and has become a dance to be viewed rather than one inviting popular participation. The national contemporary version of *zapin* faces totally different performance constraints from village *zapin*. *Zapin Melayu* and *Zapin Arab* remain as village traditions but have been rapidly losing their appeal to the younger generation and are known even less by the rest of the nation. The various forms of *zapin* belong to a common genre but

each has taken a different form and meaning. One can speak of a continuum of a genre, within which are many styles, each having different
forms.

On a much broader level, this book views the development of *zapin*
within the framework of the evolution of national Malay culture and
identity. In this context, the origins of *zapin*, its structural transformations, its changes in meaning, and its integration into a national folk
culture are viewed as symptomatic of larger changes in Malay culture.

Research on *Zapin*

The author's initial research on *zapin* covered the entire region of
Peninsular Malaysia. In 1983, his interest lay in the study of the *zapin*
dance as performed and seen live on stage and in the pre-recorded
taped versions shown on Malaysian television. The study was mainly
carried out in the urban centres, especially the state capitals, as these
centres were almost certain to contain one or more dance groups that
included *zapin* in their repertoire. The main focus of the study was the
differences in the styles of performance and the floor plans exhibited
by different dance groups.

Outside the state capitals, research was conducted by randomly
selecting towns in different states for study. Certain towns, including
some state capitals, such as Alor Star in Kedah, Kuala Trengganu in
Trengganu, Georgetown in Penang, Johore Bahru in Johore, and Kuala
Lumpur, the federal capital of Malaysia (Map 1) were found to have
a higher density of *zapin* performers than others. The research did not
cover smaller towns with youth organizations or cultural clubs that
performed *zapin* on special occasions or at formal functions.

In all of these research sites, with the exception of north-west Johore
and Kuala Trengganu, the dance groups performed the contemporary
version of *zapin* with some minor differences in styles and movements.
It seemed that the dance style and movement vocabulary adhered
to those of the National Dance Group based in the National Cultural
Complex in Kuala Lumpur. This Group appeared to exercise some
form of centralized control over dance structure and style in the rest of
the country.

In 1984, the author began looking at the stylistic differences of *zapin*
in Kuala Lumpur and the versions seen in north-west Johore and in one
particular group in Kuala Trengganu. Sensing that the Kuala Trengganu
version may have been influenced by the Johore tradition, he decided
to devote particular attention to the Johore tradition. In the same year,
his research uncovered the major differences between the contemporary version of the *zapin* genre and the one in Johore.

Two areas in Johore, Muar and Batu Pahat, have maintained a form
of the *Zapin Melayu* tradition which is not duplicated anywhere else in
the country except in Kuala Trengganu. It was in and around these
two districts that, in 1984 and 1985, the author conducted his research

MAP 1
Peninsular Malaysia, Sumatra, and Singapore

on the *zapin* tradition. He looked in particular at four towns, Lenga, Pagoh, and Muar within the Muar district and Batu Pahat in the Batu Pahat district. The first three towns are quite close to one another, while Batu Pahat is relatively close to Muar; Muar and Batu Pahat are situated on the coast (Map 2). Lenga and Pagoh are located on or near the Muar River, while Muar is on the estuary of the Muar River; Batu Pahat, also known as Bandar Penggaram, is on the Batu Pahat River not far from the coast of west Johore (Map 3). The fact that these four towns are located close to a river or coastline is a strong indicator of the possibility that they were important centres of administration, commerce, and culture in the past. The close proximity of all these towns to Malacca and their foundations as riverine townships during the early period of their history seemed, to the author, to indicate a rich and hidden source of information about the nature of the *zapin* tradition in these areas and its relationship to the contemporary *zapin* genre.

From June to September 1989, the author was able to conduct more research in Malaysia and research in Singapore and Indonesia also. This research unearthed further information on the *zapin* tradition as practised in areas which shared a common traditional and cultural background but which are located within different nation-states.

Research in Singapore was conducted mainly in the south, where most of the informants lived. Most of the male informants used to be cabaret musicians, while the females were former taxi dancers.[1] They are now elderly and live in Singapore Housing and Development Board apartments in Bedok and Geylang Serai. The younger generation of *zapin* performers are members of Malay cultural associations or clubs, the most prominent being the Sriwana Dance Troupe. During the author's period of research in Singapore, this troupe often rehearsed their dance routines at the Victoria Theatre in downtown Singapore. There were also informants from the Toa Payoh and Jurong districts.

From Singapore, the study continued in the Riau Islands, where the author focused his research on Penyengat (see Map 3), an island which is twenty minutes away by motorized *perahu*[2] from Tanjung Pinang, the commercial and administrative centre of the Riau Archipelago. Being the former site of the Riau–Malay Sultanate, which was part of the greater Johore–Riau kingdom in the eighteenth century, Penyengat is regarded as the symbolic centre of Malay culture. Although Penyengat is today the home of a small fishing community, there are also among its residents a small number of former aristocrats and members of the Tanjung Pinang administrative community. These former aristocrats include a group of *zapin* dancers and musicians. Tanjung Pinang has several groups of *zapin* performers which are affiliated to cultural associations that represent the migrant settlers who came from the neighbouring islands.

The author visited Pekanbaru, the capital of Riau Province and situated on mainland Riau, after completing research in Tanjung Pinang and Penyengat. Pekanbaru is situated upstream along the Siak River, not far from Siak Sri Indrapura, the former capital of the Siak

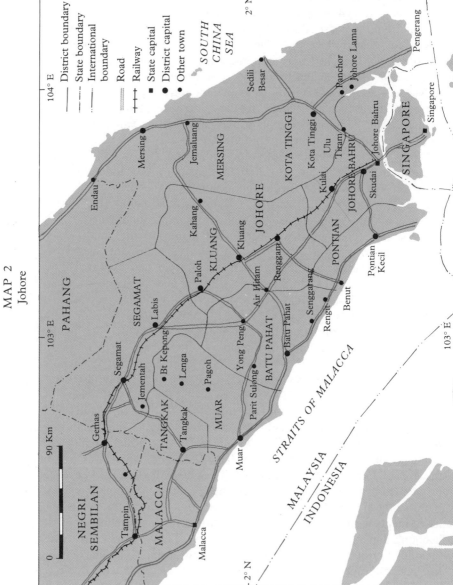

MAP 2
Johore

MAP 3
Johore and the Riau Archipelago

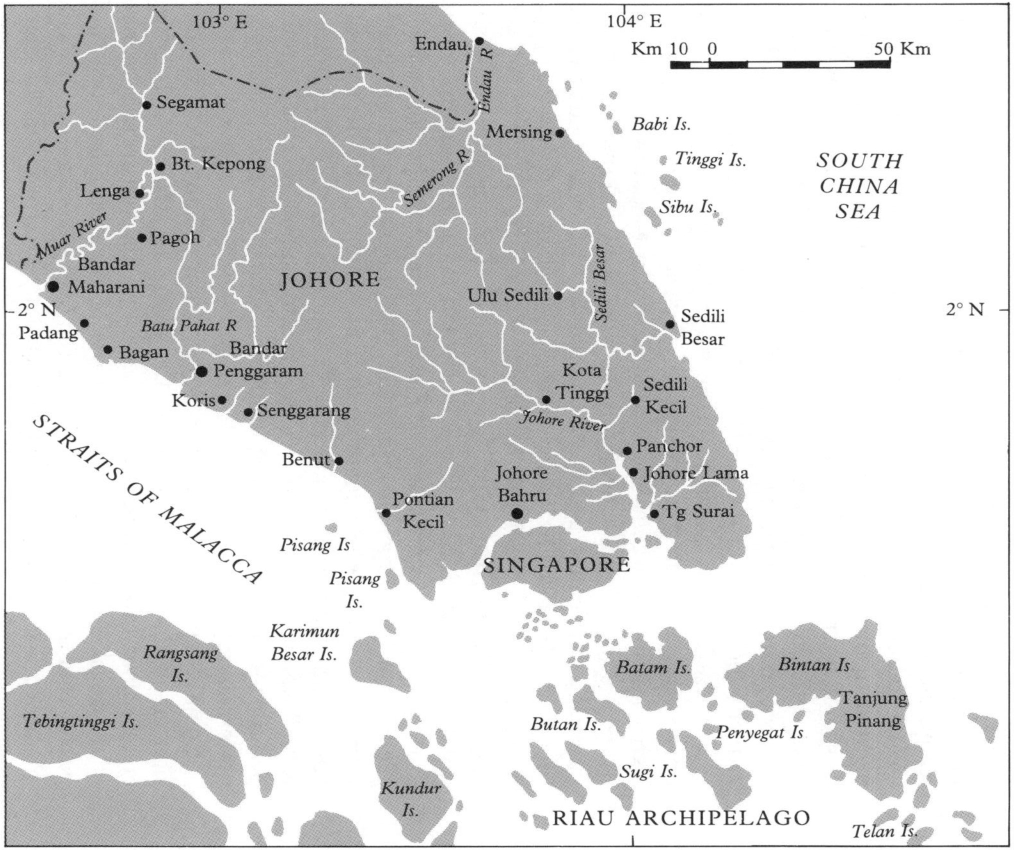

Sultanate. Although Pekanbaru has quite recently been developed by the Indonesian government into a provincial capital, it is nevertheless geographically within the territory of the former Siak Sultanate. Research on the *zapin* tradition in Pekanbaru revealed the dance style of the Siak tradition rather than a continuum of the island Riau tradition. The availability of informants, ranging from performers of *zapin*, scholars from the University of Riau, officers of the Department of Education and Culture, and royal genealogists to freelance critics of Malay culture, made Pekanbaru the most viable location for research on the styles of performance and the comparative relationship of the *zapin* traditions within the larger Riau region.

The author continued his comparative analysis on the *zapin* tradition in Medan, the provincial capital of North Sumatra. It is an important centre of commerce and administration and a place where many groups from different parts of Sumatra have come together. It has a history of continuous cultural exchanges[3] with Peninsular Malaysia. It was formerly the capital of the North Sumatran Malay Sultanate of Deli.

The University of North Sumatra, which has a department of ethnomusicology, is located in Medan. It is close to other institutions of higher learning as well as the Dewan Kesenian Medan which serves as the centre for cultural activities in the city. Many informants, including university academics and freelance scholars of Malay culture, were found in Medan. The major private institution for the Malay performing arts is the Sekolah Menengah Karawitan Indonesia, officially known as Kutab Ujana Geri. It is located in Tanjung Morawa, a short distance south of Medan. *Zapin* dance and music are compulsory subjects in the school curriculum at Kutab Ujana Geri, the only school in Medan which is a stronghold of Malay performance traditions. Students from the school usually continue their education in the department of ethnomusicology at the University of North Sumatra. The University is well known for its work on the documentation of North Sumatra performance traditions—which include the *batak*, *mandailing*, and *melayu* performance genres.

Istana Maimoon, the former royal palace of the Deli Sultanate, situated in downtown Medan, is the centre of *Melayu*–Deli art and culture. Part of the palace still houses the families of former members of the royal household, but other parts of the palace are open to the public. The palace is also the venue for performances—which include *zapin*—by a cultural group led by Tengku Sita, a well-known choreographer and dance teacher and a close relative of the last Sultan of Deli.

About one-and-a-half hour's bus ride south of Medan is the former Serdang principality. It used to be an important centre for Malay performance traditions sponsored by the Sultan of Serdang and performed in the Serdang palace. The former performers in the Serdang palace are now elderly, and live quite close to the site of the former palace. The art of *zapin* has, however, been handed down to a younger generation of performers. The *zapin* traditions in Medan, Serdang, and

Riau thus became the basis for a comparative study of the genre found in Malaysia and Indonesia.

The author eventually returned to Malaysia, to continue, in Kuala Lumpur, the research started much earlier. More informants were interviewed on the development of the *zapin* genre after independence in 1957. Among those interviewed were former performers in the entertainment parks and cabarets of the 1950s, former movie stars and dance choreographers, retired administrators from the Ministry of Culture, former movie directors, and scholars at the various institutions of higher learning residing in and around Kuala Lumpur. Visits were also paid to the P. Ramlee Memorial, the National Archives, and the university libraries to obtain more information about the development of the contemporary *zapin* tradition. Certain areas in Johore were revisited and more informants were interviewed during the remaining weeks of the research trip. An overall picture of the evolution of the *zapin* tradition eventually emerged.

Kuala Lumpur   MOHD ANIS MD NOR
December 1991

1. Female dancers employed by dance halls to dance with patrons who pay a fee for each dance or for a set period of time. They are called taxi dancers because 'such a dancer, like a taxi, is hired for the occasion' (*Webster's Unabridged Dictionary of the English Language*, New York: Portland House, 1989, p. 1457).

2. *Perahu, prao,* or *prau* refer to Malay boats. These boats were traditionally built for swift sailing with the lee side flat and balanced by a single outrigger (*Webster's Unabridged Dictionary*, p. 1146).

3. In the 1970s, Medan and Penang were declared twin cities. Cultural missions from each city, including performance troupes, make a yearly reciprocal trip to the respective host cities to perform at special annual festivals—the Medan Fair in Medan and the Pesta Pulau Pinang in Penang.

Acknowledgements

MANY people in different parts of Malaysia, Singapore, Indonesia, and the United States have given me a great deal of help in the preparation of this book. Although they are too numerous to name individually, I wish to express my deep gratitude to all of them. I am thankful to the various institutions that particularly provided me with grants for the research on *zapin*. The Vote 'F' Research Grant from the University of Malaya in Kuala Lumpur provided the initial funding for research in Johore from 1984 to late 1985. Subsequently, research conducted in 1989 was funded by the Center for South and Southeast Asian Studies of the University of Michigan, the Social Science Research Council (SSRC), and the American Council of Learned Societies (ACLS); the Center for South and Southeast Asian Studies furnished me with a Luce Foundation Research Grant while the SSRC and the ACLS awarded me a research fellowship for the International Doctoral Research Fellowship Program for Southeast Asia.

I wish to thank Dr Ariff Ahmad in Kuala Lumpur, Wak Rabu bin Harun in Lenga, Raja Sulong bin Raja Putih in Batu Pahat, and Pak Omar of Sungai Terap in Muar for giving me the opportunity to learn the *Zapin Melayu* dances in Johore. To Raja Hamzah Yunus and Raja Daud bin Raja Abu Bakar of Pulau Penyengat I owe a debt of gratitude for insights into the *zapin* of the Riau Islands. To my friends in Medan—Pak Anjang Nurdin Paitan, Yose Rizal Firdaus, Rizaldi Siagian, and Pak Ngah of Perbaungan—I am deeply thankful for their patience in providing me with all the assistance that I needed. I also owe thanks to Bapak Tenas Effendy and Amrin Sabrin of Pekanbaru for introducing me to the *zapin* of Siak Sri Indrapura.

I owe an immense debt of gratitude to Patricia Matusky-Yamaguchi from Boston, Massachusetts, for assisting me with the initial research in Johore and for encouraging me in the transcription of *zapin* music. My sincere thanks to her whole family for their hospitality and continued friendship.

I wish to express my gratitude to the professors at the University of Michigan who were very supportive of my research and writing. I am deeply grateful to Professor Judith O. Becker who gave me guidance and constructive criticisms in the course of my writing, and to Professors Peter Gosling, Karl Hutterer, Victor Lieberman, and Alton Becker for their helpful comments and suggestions on the manuscript.

Last but not least, I wish to thank my wife Ana for her patience and unending encouragement throughout the research period and during our stay in Ann Arbor. Her confidence in me was a continuous source of inspiration.

Contents

Appendices

Figures

Maps

Plates

15. An all-female *zapin* dance group performing in a linear position. Arm swaying is restricted to the right arm while the left holds the *songket* sarong in the manner of the *dagang luar* (a Bugis-derived costume adapted by Malay women in Johore).

Note

Plates 1–6 are by courtesy of the National Archives, Malaysia; 7–12 are by the author; and 13–15 are by courtesy of the National Museum, Kuala Lumpur.

1
Introduction

THE purpose of this book is to examine the historical evolution and transformation of a particular Malay dance genre from a regional into a national form. The book focuses on *zapin*, a dance form introduced into Peninsular Malaysia by Arab communities that settled in the state of Johore before the fourteenth century

This study will show how limited elements in regional culture and performing arts are transformed in the process of integration into the national popular culture. More specifically, it will examine the role of particular institutions such as the dance halls, the *bangsawan*, and the movies, both as designers and purveyors of elements of cultural forms and as performance contexts. The structural changes in performance styles will also be discussed, in particular the transformation of *zapin* from a participatory and flexible village form to a more rigidly stylized form of expression in national popular culture.

This study will cast light on the way in which the Malay identity is being reformulated and redefined through the introduction of 'alien' elements. It will also touch on the creation of a broad national identity through the incorporation of regional elements into a nationally perceived popular culture. The performing arts offer an excellent avenue through which these processes can be studied, since the arts function on an emotional level rather than on an explicitly rational one. Thus, this study will provide access to aspects of the creation of a national identity that are not approachable in other ways.

Preliminary research has shown that before it became a national folk dance tradition, the *zapin* dance genre was an exclusive tradition of the Arab–Malays (Malays of Arab descent) of Johore, the southernmost state of Peninsular Malaysia bordering Singapore.

In Johore, two forms of *zapin* are recognized: *Zapin Melayu* (Malay *zapin*) and *Zapin Arab* (Arab *zapin*); the former is performed mostly by the Malays and mixed-blood Malays of Arab descent, while the latter is performed mainly by the pure-blood Arab communities in Johore. *Zapin Melayu* originated as a result of cultural adaptation and assimilation from *Zapin Arab*. The latter is a more robust and energetic dance form, though they share a similar musical form. To the Malays *Zapin Arab* appears coarse and less refined than *Zapin Melayu*, as it does not encapsulate the complexities of Malay ethics and the Malay perception of aesthetics.

The *bangsawan* or Malay opera and, to a certain extent, the *pentas joget* or *joget* dance stage, both of which were popular in the 1930s and 1940s, were responsible for introducing *zapin* to the Malays on the west coast of Peninsular Malaysia. In Singapore, Penang, and Kuala Lumpur, entertainment parks, which had permanent public dance stages and were staffed with dance hostesses, were the main venues for *ronggeng*[1] (a combination of *joget* and *inang* dances), *mak inang* (an *inang* genre), and *zapin* dances, along with night-club or cabaret dances such as the tango, the samba, the cha-cha, and the mambo. As a social dance at these entertainment parks, *zapin* was still over-shadowed by all the Western ballroom or night-club dances. Its popu-larity remained at the village level, where it was performed during wedding feasts or other social functions.

The post-Second World War period heralded a new era for pan-Malayan folk dance traditions. The development of cinema and radio provided traditional genres with new modes of presentation and ulti-mately with new artistic values. The movie industry in the 1950s and 1960s was especially important in developing these values. Malaysians were made aware of the versatility of the folk dance as a medium for a new-found level of creativity as the songs, dances, and musicals of the cinema began drawing on the existing folk dance traditions. Indian movie directors who were brought in to direct Malay movies used the same style of directing as they had used in their home country. They introduced Indian stories and plots into the Malay cinema, making them palatable to Malay audiences by combining them with elements of dance and music from regional Malay traditions. Thus songs and dances derived from local folk dance and music traditions entered the national scene. *Zapin*, in particular, underwent a period of profoundly creative choreography. It was taken out of its traditional setting and made to serve a new musical expression, to be sung and danced by famous movie stars and even chorus lines, initiating the audience into a world of silver screen fantasies never before experienced. New dance motives introduced in the movies were eagerly imitated, changing the course of *zapin* from a folk tradition into a popular genre and blurring its humble beginnings.

The movie industry had thus penetrated the traditional geographical boundaries confining *zapin* to the north-western part of Johore and elevated it to national consciousness. The genre came to be extensively used as a dance and musical idiom for a wide variety of contexts, from Malay classical stories to modern Malay tragedies. *Zapin* in its new form eventually became known nation-wide, but only as presented on the silver screen. Today, *zapin* may be seen as an accompanying dance routine in television entertainment series.[2]

Village *zapin* has ceased to be of importance at the national level, perhaps because it has been forgotten or is considered an unknown tradition by younger Malaysians. *Zapin Melayu* is still performed for the same social functions by the people of the same areas in Johore as formerly, but it is showing signs of decay and may eventually be forgotten as well. The contemporary *zapin* of popular culture and the original village *zapin* have long ceased to be one, each having assumed a different form yet sharing a common name and a common origin.

1. *Joget* is a relatively fast-paced dance in duple or triple beat. In contrast, *inang* consists of walking motions in either relatively slow or fast tempo. *Ronggeng*, which combines both the *joget* and *inang*, was equally popular in North Sumatra in the 1930s and 1940s, and in the 1950s when singing contests between individual contenders from the audience and the *ronggeng* singers were presented on stage. They danced to the tunes of songs entitled 'Gunung Sayang', 'Lagu Dua', 'Inang', and 'Zapin' (see Chapter 4), while improvising on *pantun* or Malay quatrains.

2. The television entertainment series are locally produced and are shown on prime time television. They captivate a relatively large audience because they include popular singers who appear with a chorus of dancers, singing and dancing to the popular songs of the month.

2
Zapin in Johore

IN deciding what makes a performance genre Malay, one normally considers the paradigmatic boundary of its 'Malayness' by taking into account who performs it, when it is performed, and what function it serves in Malay *adat* or customs and, to some extent, in Islamic religious celebrations. These criteria remain the identifying factors for all Malay traditional performances. Malay chauvinism, and the necessity to construe as Malay any obscure performance phenomena which have the faintest trace of a *Melayu* element, sometimes overshadow the need to see these performances in the broader multi-ethnic perspective. The crown of Malay identity is Islam. Performances which contain Islamic and Middle Eastern elements are normally construed as being Malay and Islamic. Yet, in some instances, a Malay–Arab dichotomy is identified. This happens when a conflict in style of performance or representation of colours[1] arises and, above all, when the Malay's 'Malayness' is challenged or threatened. A case in point is the dichotomy between *Zapin Arab* and the traditional *Zapin Melayu* of Johore.

The *Zapin Melayu* genre is considered to be a manifestation of Malay–Islamic cultural evolution as seen in the interaction of Arab influences through the segregation of performers by sex (although both sexes dance together), and through its musical instruments: the *gambus* (lute or *'ud*), *marwas* hand drums, and *dok* long drum. The dominance of the *gambus* as a melodic instrument gives it a Middle Eastern flavour: Arab and Islamic. The flavour fits well with the Malay assumption that Arab material culture symbolizes Islamic culture, a major factor of Malay identity. Arab material culture is a source of authority and legitimacy in defining the realm of Malay–Islamic culture in Malaysia—it is Malay and Islamic. Perhaps this explains the exceptional prestige of the *zapin* genre among the Malay performers in Peninsular Malaysia, Singapore, the Riau Islands, and Sumatra.

The Origins of *Zapin*

In Peninsular Malaysia, Singapore, the Riau Islands, and Sumatra, *zapin* designates a performing arts genre which encompasses a repertoire of dances and a body of music. But first and foremost, *zapin* refers to a particular kind of dance usually performed by men. In his *Unabridged Malay–English Dictionary*,[2] Winstedt notes that the word *zapin* is of Arabic origin, with its most frequent usage found in the state of Johore. Wilkinson explains that *zapin* is an Arabic-derived word which denotes an Arab dance performed by two persons.[3]

Both definitions associate the *zapin* genre with an Arab-derived tradition. The consensus of the Johore, Riau, and North and East Sumatran Malays in associating the origin of the dance with the Arabs that settled in the Malay areas of maritime South-East Asia is congruent with the two definitions. The Johore Malays, in particular, attribute the development of *Zapin Arab* and *Zapin Melayu* to a dance tradition of the Hadhramis (the Arabs of Hadhramaut) who first brought the Hadhrami tradition to the Malay areas. However, none of the author's informants in Peninsular Malaysia, Singapore, the Riau Islands, and Sumatra could name the dance genre which had preceded the *zapin* tradition.

The word *zapin* may have come from the Arabic root word *zaffa* (زفّ) which means 'to lead the bride to her groom in a wedding procession'. It is important to trace *zapin* from the Arabic root word since the Arabic-derived word in the Malay vocabulary may have undergone modification in sound and taken a meaning other than the original Arabic word. This is all the more important when it cannot be directly associated with an Arab performance genre. One can only speculate on its origins from the manner in which the root word is conjugated and then try to associate the conjugated Arabic words with the word *zapin*. The Arabic word with the closest association to the root word *zaffa* is *zafah* (زفة) which means 'wedding', while *zafana* (زفن) means 'to dance at a wedding'. Wehr[4] interpreted *zafana* as 'to dance or gambol'; thus, the word is associated with some form of prancing or frolic. Lane[5] explained *zafanan* (زفنان) as 'danced, played, or sported' (كانت تزفن الحسن). A dancer is called *zaffan* (زفان). *Zafana* refers to an honoured and respected dance tradition associated with a wedding celebration.[6] The resemblance of *zapin* to *zafana* in terms of the place of performance, style of the dance, the occasion at which it takes place, and the overall Arab ambience of the musical and dance genre thus suggest the plausibility of the origin of *zapin* in a Hadhrami tradition.

It is important to understand the history of the Hadhramaut Arabs in South-East Asia since they form the largest single group of Arabs to have come to South-East Asia since the beginning of the nineteenth century.[7] The Arab population in Singapore, the Malay Peninsula, Sumatra, and Java began to increase during the nineteenth century, with the establishment of stable economic conditions in these regions. As Drewes noted, '... the imigration [*sic*] of Had[h]ramis into Indonesia is of much later date than the advent of Islam'.[8] Tibbetts attributed the Arab settlements before the fourteenth century to commercial rather than religious reasons. 'The colonies or settlements, set up at quite a few important places in South-East Asia, were the general result of this commercial activity.... These settlements were established solely for commercial reasons and it is doubtful if any Muslim missionary work was carried on.'[9]

The existence of the Arab settlements contributed to the influence of Middle Eastern cultural traditions on the local population. Indeed, the main source of Arab cultural influence in Peninsular Malaysia, Singapore, and Indonesia may not have come directly from Hejaz, the land of the holy cities of Mecca and Medina, but instead from the land of Hadhramaut.

Hadhramaut (Map 4), which is today located in the People's Democratic Republic of Yemen, is made up of a valley complex in the middle of southern Arabia and is separated from the southern coast of the Arabian Peninsula by a mountain range. In the strictest sense, Hadhramaut refers to the deep valley running parallel to the southern coast of Arabia from roughly 48° E to 50° E. Although in ancient times Hadhramaut was famous for its export of incense (such as frankincense and myrrh), the violent tribal wars (fought over water holes) which divided the people and the aridness of the landscape became major factors for the out-migration of the Hadhramis to Yemen, Syria, India, and South-East Asia. The location of Hadhramaut on the great trade route from South-East Asia to the Mediterranean coast has, since Roman times, also contributed to this out-migration of the Hadhramis. Aden, which became the port whence vessels set out for China and India in the middle of the twelfth century, was a major centre for the embarkation of Hadhramis for South-East Asia.

Meulen and Wissmann, who laid the foundation for a detailed study of Hadhramaut in 1931, mentioned the continuous flow of Hadhramis to South-East Asia. The emigrant Hadhramis accumulated wealth and fortune in Singapore, the other British Straits Settlements, and Java. Rich Hadhramis who built mosques and fine homes back in Hadhramaut but who lived in Johore, Singapore, and Java attest to the success of the overseas Arabs in South-East Asia.[10] Evidence from the Kanchu[11] records of Johore shows that 'by 1874, there was a Kongsi made up entirely of Arabs'.[12] The Kanchu records also show that the Arab traders who came to Johore during the late nineteenth century took part in large-scale economic ventures in acquiring new wealth in Johore. This indicates that the Arabs had begun to hold economic rights in Johore from the *pajak* (lease) system and the Kanchu system of land grants which would have placed them among the economically productive sector of the migrant population.

The Arabs' background, which gave them social prestige within the larger Islamic society in Johore, Singapore, and Java,[13] was an added advantage. Children born of South-East Asian mothers and Arab fathers were sent to Arab schools to be trained and taught to behave as Arabs—either the Arab schools in the wadis[14] in Hadhramaut (for those whose families could afford to send them there) or the local Arabic religious schools (for those from less well-to-do families). They were made to learn the Islamic religion as well as the manners and customs

MAP 4
The Arabian Peninsula: Hadhramaut

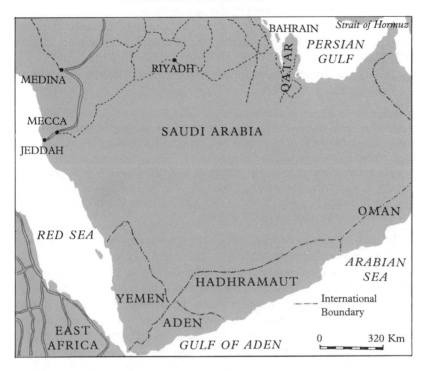

of the Hadhrami way of life. The children who eventually returned to South-East Asia from the wadis of Hadhramaut were considered better trained than their counterparts who attended local Arabic schools.

It is possible that these children born of the union of Arab fathers and indigenous mothers became the single most important factor in the bridging of the two traditions, the Arab and the indigenous. The absence of Hadhrami women in South-East Asia and the willingness of the Arabs to marry local women introduced not only a mixed race of Arab–South-East Asians but also the possibility of merged traditional values and cultures. The *zapin* tradition in Johore may well have been a result of this mix of Arab and Malay artistic expression.

It is believed that both *Zapin Arab* and *Zapin Melayu* originated from the traditions of the Hadhrami Arabs, who were known to be extremely conservative and orthodox Muslims, and that the divergence of the two forms of *zapin* was the result of a selective process of adaptation and assimilation by the Malays and Arab–Malays of Johore. *Zapin Melayu* was regarded by the Malays as more refined or *halus*[15] than *Zapin Arab*. The Malays considered themselves highly selective in adapting foreign cultural traditions and practices into their mainstream culture. *Zapin Melayu* was adapted from a more robust Arabic tradition and made to conform to the subtleties of controlled movements and the suppression of outward expressions of highly charged energy. *Zapin*

Arab, on the other hand, required high energy, with its bigger stepping motions, higher skips and jumps, wider arm sways, and more exaggerated stooping and bending of the upper torso.

Although empirical evidence of the existence of a dance tradition called *zapin* in Hadhramaut has not been found,[16] Meulen's description of a Hadhrami dance tradition perfŏrmed during a wedding celebration in 1931 gives some grounds for tracing the *Zapin Melayu* in Johore to an Arab source.

The men and women stand facing each other in long rows, which approach each other with rhythmical stamping of feet and clapping of hands and then again retreat. All [are] united in the singing of a monotonous refrain, the constant repetition of one and the same melody. The actual song is recited by a single person. They all know the old songs and enjoy taking part in them and joining in the rising enthusiasm caused by their refrain. Sweat pours down the naked chests of the men, but it is nearly morning before their energy is exhausted and the festal joy quietens down.[17]

Another account by Meulen, made during his second trip to Hadhramaut in 1939, revealed the separation of male and female guests during a Hadhrami wedding ceremony. The guests danced to the accompaniment of 'monotonous but tirelessly repeated tunes whose rhythm was accentuated by clapping of the hands while the excitement was maintained by high-throated trills (*zagharit*)'.[18] Meulen's description of male dances that he witnessed in 1939 seems to illustrate a variation found in the dances of the Hadhrami wedding celebration. One was more elegant than the other. The first dance was performed by men who held hands and danced in pairs.

... the men and youths of the village amused themselves in front of the gate and danced by the light of the lantern to the beat of a cylindrical drum.... Each was now dressed in a loin-cloth fixed by the cartridge belt that held a glittering jambiya.[19] How slender and young they looked, their dark eyes sparkling with joy and their black, greasy, curly heads uncovered! In the open space two lads danced in turn together elegantly holding each other, with hands lifted high, by the little finger. Thus they skipped up and down until a third came up behind them and presently took the place of one who retired. The onlookers marked the time by clapping their hands and often leaned forward to enjoy more fully the feminine grace of the dancers. They were not in the least bored by its unchanging monotony ... everybody was enjoying with heart and soul the rhythm and beauty of the movement.[20]

The second dance that Meulen witnessed was more of a group dance than the paired one described above. It was performed at the request of the guests and was basically meant for all to join in.

... they started a beduin dance in which all could join. They arranged themselves in two long rows facing each other, clapping hands to accentuate the time as the two ranks sang in turn. As they sang the rows started moving and now the time was also marked by stamping the feet. Gently rocking the upper part of the body the two rows [of dancers] approached each other. As the space between them became narrower and narrower the singing and stamping rose in volume. Every now and then one of the dancers would become too excited to stay in his row and would step into the narrow space between and execute a frantic solo. When the rows nearly touched they started moving back again. This dancing they can keep up for hours. The singing of the men rising and falling with the accompaniment of stamping feet formed one sonorous murmur. Occasionally a singer would lift up his voice in a high-pitched falsetto and then the monotonous song and stamping of the mass would rise like the roar of nature in storm and thunder.[21]

In the above descriptions, the only musical instrument mentioned is a cylindrical drum, which appears to be similar to the *dok* long drum of the Malay *zapin*. It is possible that the only musical accompaniment was the singing of a monotonous refrain and the rhythmic clapping of the onlookers.

There are a number of elements in the performance of *zapin* which echo the Hadhramic dance tradition. These include the linear formation of *zapin* performers who dance facing one another; the Johore dancers' practice of rhythmically stamping their feet on the fourth count of their four-beat dance phrase while tracing a recurring forward and backward floor plan; and the solo vocal accompaniment in the form of a quatrain[22] over a basic melody. The use of musical instruments consisting of the *'ud* or *gambus*, the *marwas* hand drums, and the *dok* (which sets the pace and acts as the time marker) give *zapin* a Middle Eastern flavour.

Zapin also demonstrates some modifications of the Arab *zafana* dance traditions. These include the following. The lyrics may be in Malay or Arabic or both. The vocal soloist also plays the *'ud* or *gambus*. The musicians who play interlocking patterns on their *marwas* hand drums also sing a refrain to indicate a change in the dance sequence and floor formation. The men who perform *zapin* during the later part of a Malay wedding celebration usually remain in the dance area until they succumb to exhaustion in the morning hours.

The Role of *Zapin* in Society

Zapin is a highly respected tradition among the Johore Malays, who consider it to be Arab-derived and Islamic, yet upholding Malay decency and propriety. Its purported Arab origin is seen as placing it within a performance tradition permitted by the rigorous code of Islamic conduct.

The *zapin* of Johore, Singapore, Riau, and elsewhere in Sumatra followed the Arab tradition of *zafana* in being formerly reserved for weddings and religious celebrations, and in being performed more often at weddings than at other celebrations.

In the Johore Malay wedding ceremony, the dance played a central role as an important entertainment in the evening of the wedding day. Held either on the main verandah of the house or on a specially erected platform in the courtyard of the house, *zapin* was performed by invited performers as well as by the wedding guests. The *zapin* performers were known as *penari zapin* (dancer of *zapin*) or *pemain zapin* (player of *zapin*). It was the word *zapin* which made all the difference in a performance regarded by many as a venerated tradition from the Islamic world (unlike the rest of the Malay folk dance traditions which were considered to be of lesser status and prestige).

The performers were exclusively male. Women were never expected, much less allowed, to perform the dance, although they were not barred from watching the performance from a distance behind the male spectators. This was customary practice to preserve social decency and female modesty. In the traditional manner, *zapin* was never a performance by members of both sexes. Although a night-long performance of the *zapin* was exhausting, the dance was always performed with the strictest adherence to order and decorum. The appropriateness of the dance as a wedding-related tradition required the observance of good behaviour and ceremonial etiquette on the part of dancers and spectators alike.

Zapin as a dance tradition serves both as secular entertainment and, to some extent, as religious celebration. The dance serves a secular purpose in that it is folk entertainment, where people of all ages and from all walks of life are involved directly, either as performers or audience, in a variety of locales.

Zapin's religious role is more historical. It was formerly a part of religious celebrations associated with the Maulud Nabi (Prophet Muhammad's birthday), Hari Raya Puasa (celebrated at the end of the Ramadan fasting month), Hari Raya Haji (celebrating the month of sacrifice), and Maal Hijrah (Islamic New Year). These are now highlighted by recitations from the holy Qur'ān or the singing of religious hymns from the *Kitab Berzanji*[23] and, in the past, by the performance of *zapin*. *Zapin* was the only Malay dance tradition which was allowed to be performed in and near mosques.

Although *Zapin Arab* was an exclusive tradition of the Arabs and descendants of Arab–Malays of Johore, it played a similar role to *Zapin Melayu*. *Zapin Melayu*, however, was more popular with the Johore Malays than *Zapin Arab*, being performed in villages all over north-west Johore; *Zapin Arab* was confined to proponents and admirers of purer Arab-derived culture clustered around the Arab–Malay residential areas. Sometimes both *zapin* traditions were performed at the same location especially when performers of the two traditions were invited to the same social function. Conflicts between performers of the two dance styles were virtually unknown since both traditions were assumed to be symbiotically linked to the same source.

Zapin may also be seen as a force for social cohesion at the village level, being the remuneration for the days of communal labour spent helping with the preparation for a wedding feast.

In the villages of north-west Johore, *zapin* performances were considered important events where the performers' dancing skills were openly displayed for public viewing. Because these performances normally took place during weddings or religious celebrations, it was considered proper and appropriate for normally shy and reserved individuals to show off their talents without harming their reputation in the community. A *zapin* performance held during a wedding celebration was considered an event which no member of the village should miss. It served not only as an occasion for 'people-watching' but also as an opportunity for any male member of the community to step up to the dance arena and join in the group performance of *zapin*. The dance required the ability to absorb and remember the sequences of motives being performed. Since most of the dance motives were repeated many times, in a set of sequential patterns, the dancers had the choice of joining, remaining, or leaving the dance area whenever the cycle of dance motives in a particular dance sequence was completed.

Zapin performances were also occasions when performers from similar occupations or with similar recreational interests could meet one another. It was common for performers in the bigger towns such as Muar and Batu Pahat to associate themselves with others of similar occupations such as trishaw riders, petty traders, food vendors, or boat paddlers.[24] The *zapin* performers also enjoyed the same recreational interests; they were bird trappers, soccer players, or members of recreational clubs and associations. *Zapin* provided the focus for individuals not only to meet and practise in the pursuit of performance excellence but to share and exchange new ideas in their *zapin* repertoire.

During *zapin* performances, the dancers belonging to specific occupational or recreational groups would dance together in pairs, displaying their numerous dance motives and juxtapositions of dance sequences, while tracing challenging floor plans. Groups of *zapin* performers would dance alternately or at specific intervals during the night-long performance with the tacit intention of displaying the best of dance styles from each representative fraternity. It was important to be subtle in the display of dance skills in order to maintain the respect of the hosts, the women, and the children who came to see the performance. *Zapin* is a tradition which does not tolerate competitive displays which may harm the reputation of any performer. There must always be orderliness in spite of the tacit desire to be the best performer and the best performance group. *Zapin* provided an avenue for competitive expression and at the same time it maintained comradeship and brotherhood among the performers.

Another role of *zapin* was as a leisure outlet for urban workers, a role that developed with the emergence of urban entertainment parks and dance halls during the late 1930s. *Zapin* was included in the repertoire of cabarets and dance halls patronized by migrant rural workers in the major towns in the Malay Peninsula, Singapore, and even Sumatra. *Zapin* thus took on a role different from the one that it had in the villages as a purely voluntary performance for the hosts of a wedding celebration, at a religious occasion, or for the delight of women and children. Within the commercial environment of urban entertainment parks and dance halls, *zapin* provided an outlet for rural workers to express their nostalgia for a tradition that was a part of their village roots. *Zapin* was never able to challenge the supremacy of the Western and Latin social dance genres in the entertainment parks and dance halls, but it managed to survive the onslaught of these dance crazes of the era. Even though patrons had to pay in order to perform *zapin* in the urban centres, *zapin* nevertheless remained a tradition which reminded them of their rural backgrounds while serving the commercial purpose of the dance halls and urban entertainment parks.

By the end of the Second World War, *zapin* fulfilled both the modern expectations of a changing society and the traditional artistic expressions of the Malays. It subsequently developed further to meet the needs of a new form of entertainment, the movie industry of the 1950s and 1960s, and to satisfy the nationalistic fervour, from the mid-1960s, to retain some form of national dance heritage.

The Performers of *Zapin*

Traditionally the performers of *Zapin Melayu* and *Zapin Arab* were exclusively male, but contemporary *zapin* allows participation by men and women. This change owes much to the development, since the end of the Second World War, of a more liberal perception of the degree of freedom of artistic expression permitted within the constraints of decency and propriety in Malay culture. However, there are still traditionalist performers in Johore today who comply with the one-gender tradition of *Zapin Melayu* or *Zapin Arab*. The all-male tradition in *Zapin Melayu* in Johore was broken as recently as the mid-1970s with the creation of a teenage group made up of boys and girls.

The membership of a group of traditional *zapin* performers was based upon place of domicile, occupation, or recreational interests. Just as their common background provided performers with a sense of fraternity, it also made it easy for them to meet at members' homes for practice sessions, with a more experienced member acting as the guide or dance leader; he sometimes obtained new ideas and dance motives from other groups. The organization of groups was often *ad hoc* and voluntary, with leadership alternating between members. The survival of the groups depended more on the contributions of the members than on the personality of the leaders and membership did not necessarily alter when there was a change of leadership. Contributions, in cash or kind, for the upkeep of the group's dance paraphernalia, such as items of clothing and musical instruments, were not mandatory but were encouraged. The repair of the *marwas* hand drums and the *dok* long drums was less expensive than the repair or purchase of a new '*ud* or *gambus*.

During the 1920s and 1930s, members of a *zapin* dance group were recruited from successive generations of the families of performers. A father-and-son pair was common, as was an uncle-and-cousin pair from the same extended family. The families would normally be associated through some form of social or interest association. Training would usually be held in private homes or informal club houses.

The lower age limit for performers was around puberty and there was no upper age limit. More often than not, an old and experienced musician was considered more valuable than a young teenage dancer who still had much to learn. But this did not mean that young boys were dissuaded from joining the *zapin* groups. On the contrary, the young boys in a family of performers were encouraged to learn and imitate the dance by rote so as to cultivate a sense of belonging to the group and the dance tradition. Many of the young boys were allowed to dance together in a family performance and were encouraged to show off their skills in front of family members, this being an incentive for the perpetuation of their interest in learning and practising the *zapin* with the older members of the group. Performance at occasions beyond the family was only allowed when the younger boys were considered professional performers, usually when they were in their early to mid-teens. Young men in their twenties made up the majority of traditional *zapin* performers. People in this age-group were considered the most agile and supple. They were easy to teach and were relatively eager learners. They had tremendous energy for prolonged performances and possessed a masculine grace in their dance styles. Having received training and having acquired a working knowledge of the dance from older members of *zapin* groups or individuals in their extended family, the young men were receptive to the notion of hard work and demanding hours of practice whenever they were required to represent their respective organizations.

There were many clubs and associations representing *zapin* groups. One organization active in the promotion of *zapin* in Singapore in the 1930s and 1940s was the Bawean[25] organization, called the Pondok Boyan. The Pondok Boyan, literally translated as 'Bawean Hut', represented groups of Baweanese youth from the various villages in Singapore. Young, unmarried male Baweanese were required to stay in the centralized sleeping quarters known as *pondok* or huts. These huts provided the venue for informal clubs of Bawean youths as well as for various forms of instruction. The Bawean youths were taught the finer aspects of religion, the subtleties of the movements of the Malay *silat* martial arts, and the grace of the *zapin* dance during their stay at the Pondok Boyan. In return, they were expected to uphold the good name of their *pondok* whenever they performed the *silat* or the *zapin*. The youths considered performing the *zapin* for their respective *pondok* to be a great honour. It was important for them to perform the *zapin* in the most professional way since it involved not only the pride of their respective *pondok* but also that of the Bawean people as a whole.

Another informal association of *zapin* performers comprised the aristocratic members of a *zapin* group in Kampung Koris in Pengaran in the district of Batu Pahat, Johore. Led by a Malay Raja, an aristocrat of the Johore royal house, this *zapin* group was initially made up entirely of family members of the Raja residing in and around Kampung Koris. This group was set up in the 1930s by the forebears of the present leader, Raja Sulong Raja Putih, for the purpose of promoting the traditional *Zapin Melayu* among the family members of the Raja, amongst whom *Zapin Melayu* was highly regarded as an example of fine Malay culture. To be able to perform *zapin* and play the musical instruments demonstrated taste for the finer Malay traditions. The special status ascribed to *Zapin Melayu* as a tradition which was at once Islamic and Malay legitimized the dance tradition for this circle of aristocratic performers. This group of dancers and musicians has, however, since the mid-1980s, shown signs of decline and disintegration. Younger members of the Raja's family are no longer interested in taking up the *zapin* tradition or perpetuating what was once the pride of the Raja's household.

In the area of Bakri in the Muar township, there is a group of *zapin* performers who are students in an informal religious group led by their teacher Ustaz Abu Bakar. The Ustaz[26] is also the village imam[27] and is well respected in Bakri. The students, most of whom are teenagers, perform the *zapin* whenever the community invites them to do so at wedding celebrations. The membership of the *zapin* group is voluntary but individuals who have agreed to perform on a designated date are expected to turn up for practices at the home of the Ustaz. This particular group performs a form of *Zapin Melayu* with strong influences from *Zapin Arab*, reflecting the close relationship between *zapin* and religious institutions. In Muar, there are a few other groups of *zapin* performers who are students of the Ustaz. The religious teachers are receptive to *zapin* and the tradition of teaching it to their students. Most of them believe that *zapin* serves both the secular world and the Islamic tradition. The teachers consider that *zapin* should be encouraged and continued through the generations.

Elsewhere in the Muar, Pagoh, and Batu Pahat areas of north-west Johore, *Zapin Melayu* performers since the late 1970s have represented youth organizations known as *kumpulan belia*. These organizations were set up and supported by the district offices of the then Ministry of Youth and Sports. Among the organizations' cultural events or classes, the *zapin* dance is considered to be the most suitable group activity. Since these groups are located in an area which is considered to be a stronghold of the *zapin* tradition, *Zapin Melayu* has become the prime vehicle for cultural learning. With the realization that *Zapin Melayu* is already losing its appeal among the younger generation of Johore Malays—and with the rest of the country almost oblivious to it—the *kumpulan belia* or youth organizations determined that they at least should be able to perform *Zapin Melayu* for their local communities.

If youths form the core of traditional *zapin* dancers, older men form the majority of musicians. The difficulty in training young musicians is due to either a lack of interest among the younger generation or the reluctance of the older musicians to spend time and effort teaching the younger ones, making the teaching and learning of *zapin* music an almost impossible task. The availability of recorded music[28] enables *zapin* groups to concentrate on the dancing and neglect the learning of *zapin* music. Most of the young musicians are only interested in playing the percussion instruments such as the *marwas* and the *dok*. Despite the challenging nature of the interlocking drumming patterns on the *marwas* the young musicians consider the *gambus* more difficult to learn than the *marwas*. Learning the *gambus* entails long hours of training and, above all, a willingness to be an apprentice to the *gambus* teacher, to follow him in all of his performing engagements and to run errands for him when necessary. The old musicians, on the other hand, are not eager to teach young students who, they fear, are not committed and to whom it would be a waste of time and effort to teach the basics, much less the advanced ornamentations and styles of *gambus* playing.

Another factor that prevents experienced musicians from teaching and imparting their knowledge and playing skills is that they have little leisure time for teaching. They hold full-time jobs—as school or religious teachers, trishaw riders, merchants, or farmers—since they cannot rely on *zapin* for subsistence because performances are irregular and the payments are usually nominal.

Thus it is clear that, despite the efforts of some groups to perpetuate *Zapin Melayu*, this tradition is declining. Among the reasons for this decline are the reduction in the numbers of young performers to replace the older dancers and musicians and the continued adherence to an all-male performance tradition. In comparison, performers of contemporary *zapin* are not subject to such limitations. The *zapin* of today, a result of the artistic adaptation of *Zapin Melayu* into Malay popular culture,[29] does not require strict adherence to a specific gender group of performers and is more receptive to modern innovations in both the music and the dance repertoires. The evolutionary processes that the *zapin* genre has undergone since the end of the Second World War, culminating in contemporary *zapin,* has emancipated *zapin* from the traditional role that it played in society.

Zapin has evolved into a performance to be viewed rather than one to be participated in. Performers dance the *zapin* in strict accordance with a choreographed routine and every attempt is made to ensure that there are no mistakes in performing difficult dance movements. The dancers practise at regulated hours and perform at functions other than wedding celebrations. Schoolchildren and youths form the majority of the performers of contemporary *zapin*. Mixed-gender participation has become the norm. Nevertheless, contemporary *zapin* dancers still maintain the separation of the sexes during performances, and members of the opposite sex dance past each other either in pairs or in opposing linear formations. There is no physical contact through the holding of hands or the touching of any part of the partner's anatomy. The liberty in performance style and the participation of performers are subjected to the same traditional values of social decency and propriety as in *Zapin Melayu*.

Contemporary *zapin* is more popular than *Zapin Melayu*, primarily because the Malaysian public generally is more aware of it. To the average Malaysian, *zapin* is synonymous with the contemporary version. It is taught in schools, youth organizations, community centres, college and university campuses, and in private homes. More people know how to perform contemporary *zapin* than *Zapin Melayu*. Contemporary *zapin* serves the aspiration of nation-building as one of the national dance traditions of Malaysia. It is not village-centric like *Zapin Melayu* and is not resistant to modern innovations. Nevertheless, contemporary *zapin* does owe its origins to *Zapin Melayu*. Although both belong to one genre, each has its own form.

1. Green and black are colours which are normally associated with Islam in Malaysia. Green is by far the most popular colour worn by men while black is more popular with women. Not every Malay Muslim in Malaysia wears these colours—only the conservative and fundamentalist few—as symbolic representations of the Islamic *ummah* or Islamic community.

2. Richard Winstedt, *An Unabridged Malay–English Dictionary*, 6th edn. (Kuala Lumpur: Marican, 1965).

3. R. J. Wilkinson, *A Malay–English Dictionary (Romanised)* (London: Macmillan & Co. Ltd., 1959).

4. Hans Wehr, *A Dictionary of Modern Written Arabic*, ed. J. Milton Cowan (Wiesbaden: Otto Harrassowitz, 1961), pp. 378–9.

5. Edward William Lane, *An Arabic–English Lexicon* (Beirut, Lebanon: Libraire du Liban, 1980), pp. 1237–8.

6. Dance in this context cannot be associated with *raqasa* (رقص), a term which implies folk dancing, and other forms of dancing as well, but in a less respected and less honoured gathering than a wedding. The association of gaiety and happiness in a wedding dance does not, however, concur with the general notion of *raqasa* which is sensuous, sexy, and cheap. A father is said to be proud to have his daughter dance at a wedding but not at a *raqasa*. *Raqasa* are performed in entertainment clubs or establishments which solicit money from patrons. (Sa'd al-Khadim, *Al-Raqs al-Sha'bi fi Misr*, al-Qahirah [Cairo]: Al-Hay'ah al-Misriyah al-'Ammah lil-Kuttab, 1972.)

7. William R. Roff, 'The Malayo–Muslim World of Singapore at the Close of the Nineteenth Century', *Journal of Asian Studies*, Vol. XXIV, No. 1 (1964), p. 81.

8. G. W. J. Drewes, 'New Light on the Coming of Islam to Indonesia?', in Ahmad Ibrahim, Sharon Siddique, and Yasmin Hussain (eds.), *Readings on Islam in Southeast Asia* (Singapore: Institute of Southeast Asian Studies, 1985), pp. 7–17.

9. G. R. Tibbetts, 'Early Muslim Traders in South-East Asia', *Journal of the Malayan Branch of the Royal Asiatic Society*, Vol. XXX, Part I (Singapore: MBRAS, 1957), p. 44.

10. D. Van Der Meulen and H. Von Wissmann, *Hadramaut: Some of Its Mysteries Unveiled* (Leyden: E. J. Brill, 1964), p. 93.

11. The Kanchu system, devised in the 1840s in Johore by Temenggung Ibrahim, the first ruler of modern Johore, was a system of land grants.

12. Carl A. Trocki, *Prince of Pirates: The Temenggongs and the Development of Johor and Singapore 1784–1885* (Singapore: Singapore University Press, 1979), p. 175.

13. 'The Malays had for centuries tended to look upon all Arabs, whatever their origins, as direct inheritors of the wisdom of Islam, and on Sayyids in particular (decendants of the Prophet) as possessed of unexampled piety and religious merit. Many of the Hadhramis who came to the East in the nineteenth century were, in fact, cultivated and scholarly men in an ancient tradition, with their roots in a literary and religio-legal society which has been likened, in its institutions and manners, to those prevailing in the centers of medieval Islam. In the East Indies, as in their own land, the Sayyids and Shaykhs of the Hadhramaut and those descended from them formed a respected, influential, and often wealthy class, somewhat set apart from their fellows.... Best known as traders and merchants, they formed the elite of the Islamic community in Malaya and Indonesia.' (Roff, op. cit., pp. 81–2.)

14. A wadi is a valley in the desert. The wadis in Hadhramaut may also contain oases which serve as the primary sources of water in the desert.

15. *Halus* includes the notion of *murni* (pure, clean, and harmonious), *lembut* (soft, kind, polite, graceful, and gentle), and *budi-pekerti* (cultured character).

16. Although there are no known records of dance traditions in Hadhramaut by the name of *zapin*, there is overwhelming consensus among the South-East Asian informants that *zapin* originated from Hadhramaut.

17. Meulen and Wissmann, op. cit., p. 29.

18. D. Van Der Meulen, *Aden to the Hadhramaut: A Journey in South Arabia* (London: John Murray, 1947), pp. 47–8.

19. A *jambiyah* is a short dagger usually in a silver sheath often adorned with red semi-precious stones and stuck in the waistband. Ibid., p. 244.

20. Ibid., p. 48.

21. Ibid.

22. The quatrains are known as *pantun* which are composed to fit into a song pattern of a four-lined stanza containing a *pembayang maksud* (foreshadow of the intention) in the first two lines and the *maksud* (intention) in the last two lines. An example of a *pantun* is as follows:

(Malay text)

Buah cempedak di luar pagar	pembayang maksud
Ambil galah tolong jolokkan	pembayang maksud
Saya budak baru belajar	maksud
Kalau salah tolong tunjukkan	maksud

(English translation)

Jackfruits hang outside the fence	foreshadow of the intention
Take a pole and knock them low	foreshadow of the intention
I have just started learning	intention
When I'm wrong please let me know	intention

The above excerpt of a *pantun* is taken from Francois-Rene Daillie, *Alam Pantun Melayu: Studies on the Malay Pantun* (Kuala Lumpur: Dewan Bahasa dan Pustaka, Ministry of Education, 1988) pp. 75–6.

23. A book containing the Muslim hymns to be recited in praise of the Prophet Muhammad.

24. The boat paddlers were one of the economically prosperous groups which supported and financed *zapin* performances in Muar. Their monopoly over the river crossings, when the only means of crossing the Muar River was by paddled boats, assured them a substantial hold on the local economy. When a permanent bridge was constructed over the Muar River in the 1960s, they lost their monopoly and subsequently their role as *zapin* financiers.

25. The Baweanese were originally from the island of Bawean situated in the Java Sea. The nearest Javanese port is near Geresik, to the west of Surabaya. The Baweanese, known throughout Malaysia and Singapore as Orang Boyan, worked as domestic helpers (females) and horse jockeys (males) in the urban areas of British Malaya and Singapore. They were also diligent plantation workers in the rubber estates during the colonial

period. The migration of the Baweanese from their island home in search of better economic opportunities and living conditions in Malaya and Singapore was instrumental in the establishment of strong pockets of Baweanese villages near major towns and cities. In Singapore, a large majority of the Baweanese worked in the services sector but kept their patterns of village organization. The Pondok Boyan were important to the young Baweanese males for the preservation of Baweanese identity and as centres of religious and cultural learning.

26. Islamic religious teachers are addressed as *ustaz* (male) and *ustazah* (female) by the Malay community.

27. An imam is a person who leads or conducts prayer services. He is usually informally appointed during a prayer session. Any adult male of sound mind can be elected imam. However, the village imam is formally appointed either by the congregation or by the district religious office and is normally a person with an adequate training in or knowledge of Islam.

28. Recordings of some traditional *zapin* songs have been commercially produced by music stores in Muar. The songs were recorded at live performances during weddings or religious celebrations and were edited by the store owners. Almost all these tapes have a high level of noise interference. Better quality recordings of the songs that accompany contemporary *zapin* have been produced by leading recording companies such as WEA and EMI. Although the contemporary songs are not entirely appropriate as an accompaniment to the traditional *zapin* dance, traditional *zapin* groups in Muar and Batu Pahat have adapted some aspects of their dance to this music. This has resulted, to a certain degree, in the blending of traditional *zapin* movements with those of contemporary *zapin*.

29. Malay popular culture implies the notion of an urban-based diffusion of indigenous and Western-derived performances and artistic expressions. It is the culture of the largely urban or metropolitan Malay society that patronizes cultural events.

3
Zapin and the Malay World

THE spread of the *zapin* tradition throughout Peninsular Malaysia into some parts of southern Thailand, Singapore, the east coast of Sumatra, the islands of Riau, and the Malay-dominated coastal areas of Borneo (including Brunei, some parts of Sarawak and Sabah, and Kalimantan) reflects the close relationship between the maritime Malays and Islam. It is of interest that the *zapin* tradition can be found only among the Muslim Malays who have had historical contacts with the Arabs and Arab culture. It is possible that some Malays may have borrowed or developed the *zapin* tradition after observing it in another Malay group.

Although *zapin* performance styles among the numerous groups of Malays in South-East Asia vary, the musical accompaniment and the basic dance phrases remain almost the same in form. The universal elements in the *zapin* tradition that are most apparent are the predominance of the *gambus* or *'ud* as the leading instrument, the use of the *marwas* hand drums and their interlocking drumming patterns, the improvised free-metred prelude dominated by the solo *gambus* player, the coda (peculiar to the *zapin* tradition), the four-beat basic dance phrase, and the absence of leg movements at the first dance count of the basic dance phrase. No other known Malay dance tradition in South-East Asia demonstrates such consistency over such a wide geographic area.

Certain societal prerequisites constrain participation in the world of *zapin* patronage. The first is the dominance of Islam as the sole system of belief in *zapin* societies. Other elements are the use of the Malay language as the lingua franca, a common historical background, the common aristocratic background of the ruling class, and the shared conceptual world of *alam Melayu* (which literally means the Malay world) as a common world-view or *weltanschauung*.

The region where the popularity of *zapin* is most obvious is the Straits of Malacca. The *zapin* tradition in this region seems to have a similar performance style to that of the former Malay political centres, to which it has ties. In Malaysia, the coastal area of north-west Johore is the centre of the *zapin* tradition. This area was at one time under the political hegemony of the Malacca empire (*c.*1400–1511). It is from this region that *zapin* is believed to have later spread to the outlying areas east and west of the Straits of Malacca. The fall of Malacca was followed by the emergence of the Johore–Riau kingdom into the Malay world and a continuation of the Malacca lineages in other parts of the Straits of Malacca region. Singapore and the Riau Islands were historically tied to the greater Johore empire when *zapin* made its appearance in these areas. West of the Straits of Malacca, along the shores of the coast of East Sumatra, the Deli and Serdang Sultanates were as important as the Siak Sultanate had been in the patronage of the *zapin* tradition.

In Indonesia today, Riau Province has declared *zapin* the official state dance tradition.[1] By contrast, in the 1980s North Sumatra tried without much success to have *zapin* declared one of the official state dance traditions.[2] In Malaysia, there is an unofficial consensus that *zapin* is a tradition of Johore. Elsewhere in Brunei and Kalimantan, the *zapin* tradition became associated with indigenous Islamic culture. These areas were no less important than the areas along the Straits of Malacca in promoting *zapin* as a state tradition. However, its spread from one area to another in the Straits of Malacca region is, perhaps, far more dynamic than in any other areas of insular South-East Asia.

Before the advent of colonialism in Indonesia and Malaysia, *zapin* spread in Sumatra, the Riau Islands, Singapore, and Johore through the practice of crossing the Straits of Malacca, whether for trade or for the purpose of labour migration or because of the exodus of members of the Malay ruling class due to wartime defeats or conquests. To retrace the development of *zapin* in the areas around the Straits of Malacca, it is important to look into the historical milieux of the Malay Sultanates and their contribution to the spread and establishment of the *zapin* tradition. The spread of *zapin* to become a universal tradition of the Muslim Malays in Sumatra, Singapore, and Malaysia owes much to the historical development of the region following the advance of Islam with the coming of Arab traders, and especially after the fall of Malacca in 1511 to the Portuguese.

The Historical Perspective

There is historical evidence for the assumption by the Johore Malays that the source of the *zapin* tradition lies somewhere between the Pagoh and Lenga districts (see Map 2) in an area close to the Muar River. The fall of Malacca to the Portuguese in 1511 may have marked the beginning of the *zapin* tradition in the upper reaches of the Muar River. When the Portuguese expedition against Malacca succeeded on 10 August 1511,[3] the defeated ruler of Malacca, Sultan Mahmud Shah, took refuge along the upper reaches of the Muar River, possibly in the vicinity of the Pagoh area which was then under Malacca rule.[4] The Pagoh area had long been one of the Sultan's places of retreat from court duties and official engagements. It was famous for its abundance of wild game and became one of the Sultan's favourite hunting grounds.

Zapin performers in the Lenga and Pagoh areas believe it quite likely that the Sultan's entourage included a few courtiers who may have been palace musicians or dancers in Malacca. Some informants in the Lenga and Muar areas believe that the *zapin* dance was introduced from Malacca.[5] But the absence of any evidence in Malacca today of the *zapin* dance style as observed in the Lenga, Pagoh, Muar, and Batu Pahat areas of north-west Johore seems to suggest two possibilities. The first is that the dance never took root in Malacca and was instead developed and perpetuated by the Johore Malays themselves. The second possibility is that the dance developed in Malacca through the influence of the Arab traders and entrepreneurs but all traces of it were lost when the last reigning Sultan fled to the Muar district. The eventual downfall of Malacca as the centre for Islamic learning following the Portuguese conquest may have caused the departure of learned Arabs and Malays as well as performers and admirers of *zapin* to other areas along the Straits of Malacca. Whatever the possibilities suggest, north-west Johore is the only area where *zapin* may be traced to the period of the demise of the Malacca empire.

It is believed that the *zapin* tradition was introduced into the Riau Islands when Sultan Mahmud Shah had to flee from Muar to the island of Bintan in the Riau–Lingga Archipelago. On Bintan, the Orang Laut gave political support to the Sultanate. The accounts from *Sejarah Melayu*[6] describe the friendly nature of the Orang Laut[7] in the Riau–Lingga Archipelago. They helped Sultan Mahmud Shah to escape to Kampar in Sumatra in 1526 when the Portuguese invaded Bintan. Although Sultan Mahmud Shah of Malacca died in Kampar the same year, his son Sultan Alauddin Riayat Shah was able to establish a royal court in the upper reaches of the Johore River between 1530 and 1536.[8] This was the beginning of the kingdom of Johore. Perhaps this was also the beginning of the introduction of *zapin* into the northern areas of the Riau–Lingga Archipelago.

By 1636, Johore had begun an alliance with the United Netherlands Chartered East India Company or the Vereenigde Oostindische Compagnie (VOC). Johore assisted the VOC in the assault on Portuguese Malacca which resulted in the Dutch siege of Malacca and the granting of territorial protection to Johore by the Dutch. The Dutch also initiated a peace treaty between Johore and Aceh (located north of North Sumatra Province) in 1641, which ended the hostilities between the two parties and allowed the former to concentrate on building an entrepôt and to become the centre for Islamic education. However, during the reign of Sultan Iskandar Muda of Aceh, the Acehnese, during their attempted raid on the kingdom of Johore–Riau, attacked Deli Tua, which was part of the kingdom of Aru. Deli Tua was constantly fought over by Aceh and Johore. Around 1720, a successionist war in East Sumatra, reflecting the schism in the Deli Sultanate, led to the formation of the Serdang Sultanate.[9] The formation of new sultanates and the contraction of the former territories among the Malay principalities in East Sumatra and in the Malay Archipelago

facilitated the spread of Malay customs and traditions from one principality to another. This was also the period for the expansion of
Malay–Islamic cultural values and traditions—including *zapin*—among
the Malay states within the Johore territory.

The Malacca succession in the Johore royal household came to an
end with the assassination of Sultan Mahmud of Johore in 1699 by a
group of Malay nobles. The next ruler of Johore was the Bendahara,[10]
who took the title of Sultan Abdul Jalil Shah. The legitimacy of his line
was challenged and a period of political conflict ensued, culminating in
the capture of the Johore capital in Riau in 1718 by Raja Kecil, a
contender for the Johore throne, and the flight of Sultan Abdul Jalil
Shah to Trengganu on the east coast of the Malay Peninsula. By 1719,
the kingdom of Johore was partitioned into three: 'Trengganu and
Pahang under Sultan Abdul Jalil of Johore; Siak, Bengkalis, and Batu
Bahara under Raja Kecil; and Selangor, Kelang, and Linggi under
Daeng Marewa and Daeng Manompok.'[11]

The arrival of Sultan Abdul Jalil Shah in Trengganu in 1718 marked
a new beginning in the historical relationship between Trengganu and
Johore. The relationship was further strengthened when the Sultan's
brother, Sultan Zainal Abidin, was installed as the first ruler of Trengganu
in 1722. The strength of the relationship was demonstrated by the
protection bestowed by Sultan Sulaiman Badrul Alam Shah of Johore
on the heir to Sultan Zainal Abidin's throne.

Following his death eleven years later, his youngest son, Raja Mansur, was
taken under the protection of Sultan Sulaiman of Johor. Raja Mansur was
brought up in the Johor court and later married Sulaiman's daughter. When
the young prince came of age in 1741, Sulaiman installed him as Trengganu's
second ruler.[12]

The continuation of the relationship between the states also proved
to be crucial in the spread of Malay–Islamic traditions to Trengganu.
Along with the royal entourage and exchanges of learned Islamic
scholars between Johore and Trengganu, performance traditions were
also introduced from Johore into Trengganu.[13]

The Spread of the Tradition and the Development of Variants

The close interrelationships that have existed between all the Malay
principalities on both sides of the Straits of Malacca from the period of
the downfall of the Malacca empire is reflected in their interrelated
aristocratic families. Where new principalities grew out of an old one
and old principalities merged into a bigger political grouping, inter-
marriages between the ruling families became a major force for political
loyalty and administrative stability. Almost all of the Malay principalities
have family connections with one another. The aristocrats of Perak,
Pahang, Trengganu, and Johore today can be traced to the old Malacca
nobility. Intermarriages between the Malay royal families of these states

are as common today as in the past. Prior to the breakup of the Malay world into two separate entities by the colonial powers in 1824, inter-marriages between the princes and the princesses of the Malay sultanates across the Straits of Malacca were common. Exchanges of royal brides between Trengganu and Riau, Siak and Johore, and aristocrats from the Deli, Serdang, and Langkat palaces and those in the Malay Peninsula were also common.

The tradition of consolidating power and prestige through royal affinities has also contributed to the spread of traditions between royal households. It was common practice for the bride's family to send attendants to accompany her to the residence of the bridegroom. The accompanying entourage may have consisted of several *inang pengasuh* (wet nurse), *dayang-dayang* (lady-in-waiting), or *pendayangan* (woman attendant in a palace). Sometimes, palace entertainers were also included in the royal entourage. Malay princes were normally accompanied to the bride's residence by several *hulubalang* (royal guards), and the royal entourage was also sometimes accompanied by musicians and entertainers from the bridegroom's palace. Wherever the royal couple eventually resided, their personal bodyguards, palace attendants, and entertainers usually remained with them.[14] In this manner, new performances were introduced into the palaces of the royal couple.[15] Whether the traditions remained or were short-lived depended very much upon the responses of the head of the royal household.

The *zapin* tradition found today on the island of Penyengat in Riau is believed to have been brought to the Riau Archipelago from the area of Muar in Johore. Although there is no documentary evidence as to the exact date of the advent of the *zapin* tradition in the islands, many performers in Penyengat today assume that it was first taken to the island of Bintan when Sultan Mahmud Shah had to flee Portuguese harassment in Muar shortly after the downfall of Malacca in 1511. If these accounts are true, the refugee monarch can also be credited with the introduction of *zapin* into Sumatra when he finally fled to Kampar.

A most important element in the *zapin* tradition of Penyengat is the patronage that the genre received from subsequent Malay monarchs of Riau–Lingga. *Zapin* was the tradition that was most often performed for the entertainment of the aristocrats in the Sultan's palace. Although no known records can be found indicating that *zapin* in Johore was ever performed in the company of aristocrats, the fact of royal patronage in Penyengat indicates that *zapin* may not have been simply an ordinary folk tradition. The descendants of *zapin* performers living today in the village of Kampung Bulang, on the island of Penyengat, carry the royal title Raja (King) before their names. This suggests that the *zapin* performers themselves belonged to the aristocratic class. The remaining group of *zapin* performers on Penyengat is from the family of Raja Daud bin Raja Abu Bakar, himself a keen *zapin* dancer. The oldest member of the *zapin* group is the *gambus* player, Raja Mahmud, who learned the art of *gambus* playing from the circle of aristocratic families when he was a young man. The continuity of the Raja family members in performing *zapin* suggests that *zapin* was a tradition up-held and promoted by the members of the ruling class themselves.

Evidence of a strong common element in the *zapin* tradition is in the dance style. The *zapin* dance styles of Penyengat are very similar to those of Muar and Lenga in Johore. The terminology used to identify some dance motives in the Penyengat *zapin* is also similar to that used in Muar, Lenga, and on the east coast of Sumatra. The most common terms are *titi batang*, *ayak-ayak*, *loncat tiong*, *pusa belanak* or *loncat belanak*, and *tahtim*.[16] All the terms for *zapin* dance phrases are named after stylized gestures which simulate actions of men or nature. In the *titi batang* dance motive, dancers move in the manner of crossing a bridge (*titi*) made out of a tree trunk (*batang*). *Ayak-ayak* represents a dance movement that is symbolic of one sieving sago flour. *Loncat tiong* is a movement which imitates the jumps and leaps (*loncat*) of the hill myna bird (*tiong*). *Pusa* or *loncat belanak* refers to the twirling (*pusar*) or leaps of the *belanak* fish commonly found on muddy river banks. *Tahtim* is the coda to the *zapin* dance. The use of similar terms to depict identical movements or a variation of identical dance motives in other parts of East Sumatra suggests that the *zapin* tradition spread together with Islam and the political hegemony of the Malacca–Johore empire.

The dance styles of Penyengat are also found in other districts in the Riau Province of Sumatra. The districts of Kampar, Bengkalis, Indragiri, and areas around the provincial capital Pekanbaru all include the Penyengat dance motives, together with other dance motives, in their repertoires.

A brief description of these dance motives may serve to illustrate the nature of some of the similarities. Common to all these districts is the convention of segmenting the *zapin* genre into three sections. The first section of the dance comprises salutational dance motives known as *salam pembukaan* (introductory greetings) made towards the audience. These movements consist of delivering the traditional Malay greeting with both hands clasped in front of the forehead, a gesture made at the beginning and end of an audience with a king, a sultan, or an heir to a throne. The second section consists of movements of the *zapin* proper. These dance phrases include all the Penyengat *zapin* motives as well as others categorized under the *alif* (the first alphabet of the Arabic script), *pecah* (breaks or fragmentations), *langkah* (steps or strides), *sut* (possibly an adaptation of the sound of the fourteenth letter of the Arabic alphabet but which otherwise has no meaning), *ayam patah* (chicken with a broken leg), or *tahto* (the adaptation of *tahtim* or coda) variety. These are all variations on a basic dance motive.[17] The third section forms a coda to the dance.

Informants in Pekanbaru suggested that most of the additional dance motives and their variations came from the kingdom of Siak Sri Indrapura, the former Malay kingdom of the Siak Sultanate which was founded by Raja Kecil, the Malay ruler who sought the Malacca–Johore throne after the death of Sultan Mahmud of Johore in 1699.

Since the site of the former Siak Sultanate is today located in the district of Bengkalis, it is assumed that most of the *zapin* motives are derived from the Siak version rather than that of Riau–Lingga in Penyengat.

An important factor in strengthening and promoting Arab derived customs and traditions, especially *zapin*, was the establishment of an Arab–Malay aristocratic lineage. In this connection it should be noted that, by the end of the eighteenth century, a part-Arab by the name of Sayid Ali had become the ruler of Siak.[18] He took the royal title Sultan Assyaidis Sharif Ali Abdul Jalil Shaifuddin and became the first Sultan of Siak of Arab–Malay ancestry. It was during his reign that Siak was able to expand her territory to include twelve additional colonies,[19] on the east coast of Sumatra.

The role of the Hadhramis in the spread of *zapin* is also vital. The Hadhramis, already known for their trading capabilities, were an influential trading group often accorded special commercial privileges by Malay rulers because they were considered to be of the same race as the Prophet.[20] Perhaps the Hadhramis were also responsible for the development of the Siak version of *zapin* after the crowning of Sayid Ali as the eighth Sultan of Siak. There is a possibility that the extension of the Siak *zapin* repertoire was a result of the special relationship between the reigning Sultan and his heirs and the Hadhrami traders. The Hadhramis may have provided Siak *zapin* performers with new ideas for the creation of and innovation in dance motives and phrases for their repertoire.

An important element in the relationship between the aristocrats and *zapin* dance is the *salam pembukaan* (greetings and salutations) dance motive. This motive is rarely performed in Malay folk dance traditions unless aristocrats or state dignitaries are present. It is performed to show respect and to honour special guests. Variants of the *salam* dance motive exist in the Deli and the Serdang *zapin* traditions, and the *salam* gesture is also found in the *zapin* of Johore and Riau. Perhaps the use of this particular gesture provides further proof of the relationship between *zapin* and the Malay royal houses. It is quite possible to postulate on the role of the *istana* (palace) in the spread of the *zapin* tradition in East Sumatra.

The opening dance motive of the *salam pembukaan* contains a stylized version of the introductory form of greeting by a commoner to the ruler. Although *salam* motives vary in style from one region to another, all of them are performed in accordance with the strict code of etiquette of paying homage or obeisance to Malay royalty, as in the truly traditional Malay *menyembah* (salutation or obeisance) practised in the *adat istiadat diraja Melayu* (Malay royal customs and traditions).[21] The *salam* dance motive is performed in accordance with one of the three ways of *menyembah*, as described by Alwi bin Sheikh Alhady:

(a) To the reigning monarch: Bring the hands together and, with fingers closed and palms touching, raise them to the forehead until the tips of the thumbs touch the forehead between the eyebrows. (b) To either the Yang Di-Pertuan

Muda or the Raja Muda [Heir-Apparent]: With hands and fingers as above, raise the hands in the same manner, till the tips of the thumbs touch the tip of the nose. (c) To the Bendahara or Temenggong: Similarly as above, raise the hands till the tips of the thumbs touch the tip of the chin.[22]

Although none of the *zapin* groups interviewed could explain conclusively why one particular style of *menyembah* was chosen for their dance repertoire, the general opinion was that the style of *menyembah* represented the era when *zapin* was often performed for the Sultans, the *anak-anak raja* (children of royal descent), and other aristocratic members in the *istana* (palace). This suggests that the spread of the *zapin* tradition along the east coast of Sumatra has to do with the patronage of the Sultans.

The royal palace was not only the venue at which the most talented *zapin* troupe members performed, but also the source of financial support. The most recent era of royal patronage of *zapin* in Sumatra can be traced to the Deli and Serdang Sultanates in the present Province of North Sumatra. The Sultan of Serdang was the only Malay ruler in the late nineteenth century to have an interest in the promotion of Malay performance traditions.[23] Sultan Sulaiman Shariful Alamshah, who was installed as the Serdang ruler in 1881 at the age of eighteen, introduced performances from other parts of the Malay world into the palace of Serdang. During the last decade of the nineteenth century, Sultan Sulaiman invited a group of Malay *mak yong*[24] performers from the Malay Peninsula[25] and a group of *wayang kulit* (shadow puppet) performers from the *kraton* (palace) of Yogyakarta in Java to his palace, and had established his own *bangsawan* (Malay opera) troupe called Indian Ratu.[26] The *bangsawan* performers received a fixed monthly salary from the Sultan and even toured Malaya, Singapore, and Java. The royal patronage bestowed by Sultan Sulaiman encouraged the performers of other Malay performance traditions to seek the Sultan's blessings and patronage. This the Sultan gave, to the delight of performers in Serdang.[27]

Zapin was already a well-known dance among the Deli–Serdang Malays by 1881. It was performed during social celebrations which had some religious significance, that is, on auspicious days of the Muslim calendar, such as the Prophet's birthday. *Zapin* competitions were held in the Sultan's palace, with trophies for the winners. The Sultan's favourite groups were often commanded to perform for his guests at the palace. The *zapin* groups were known as *kumpulan tari gambus* which means groups of *gambus* (*'ud*) dancers. The Sultan would invite the performers to perform before him in the audience hall. He would sit on his Kepala Gajah (Elephant's Head) throne and insist that both musicians and dancers be clearly visible from his throne.

The palace of Serdang also had its own *zapin* group known as Gambus Jamratul 'Uz. Led by Sultan Sulaiman, the group was under the close supervision of Tengku Gambus who was appointed by the Sultan to look after the well-being of the performers. The leading *marwas* player was Wak Pian who had come from Penang. The dance master was Haji Razali, who was originally from Java but who had spent twelve years of his younger days in Mecca and Hadhramaut. It was not known whether Haji Razali's sojourn in Hadhramaut had contributed to the *zapin* dance repertoire. The men were required to practise hard and were not allowed to advance to more complicated dance phrases until the Sultan himself was satisfied.

The continuity of the *zapin* tradition in Serdang from the late nineteenth century to the 1930s is illustrated in the recollections of a former *zapin* performer. In the 1930s, there were numerous *zapin* competitions known as *kongres*. It was during these *kongres* that *zapin* groups from Medan, Deli, Langkat, Binjei, and Labuhan would converge on Serdang. Winning the *kongres* was the main obsession of the Gambus Jamratul 'Uz from the Serdang palace. Penghulu Ngah, the oldest surviving former *zapin* performer in the Serdang palace of Sultan Sulaiman, vividly describes the royal command performances in their heyday in the 1930s:

We performed for Tuanku [His Royal Highness] at least twice a month. *Gambus* was his favourite performance. There was a dance arena in a square box space in front of the throne. From the Kepala Gajah, Tuanku made sure that he could see all the players. The musicians, Wak Pian, Alang, Ja'apar Buta [Blind Ja'apar], Noh, and Mail, who were *peningkah* [drummers], and Tengku Tobo sat facing the Sultan. We entered through the sides. No one was allowed to show their backs to the audience. The box where we performed was fenced and tied with yellow cloth. It was an honour to perform for Tuanku but it was scary. Tuanku was a tough disciplinarian. We had to practise hard. Whenever we emerged champions in a competition, Tuanku would throw us a party that went on for two days and two nights. We ate *roti jala* [netted pancake] and curry and danced *ronggeng*. It was fantastic then. (Translation by the author.)

The continuity of the tradition in present-day East Sumatra and Johore is striking. Not only are the dance motives in Serdang today similar to the ones in Riau and Siak, the musical instruments are also similar. The *gambus* or the *'ud* is the leading instrument, and it is accompanied by the harmonium, three or four *marwas*, a tambourine, and a *markas* (maraca). The *zapin* songs are also identical, the most popular being 'Anak Ayam' (Chicks) and 'Lancang Kuning' (Yellow Yacht). Each song begins with the *gambus* playing a non-metred solo as a prelude and ends with the interlocking sounds of the *marwas* drums. Variations in the floor plans and dance choreography *zapin* dance repertoire are often based on the songs that accompany the dance. Thus, the *zapin anak ayam* or *zapin lancang kuning* are the *zapin* performed to the songs of a similar title.

Although it is widely known that *zapin* in East Sumatra and the Riau Islands was formerly performed in and near the Sultan's palace, the genre was never limited to the palace alone. Even after the 1945 anti-royalist revolution in Sumatra, *zapin* remained popular with the common people. This suggests that the dance tradition had gained strong public support even before the demise of the Sultans' power and prestige in East Sumatra. *Zapin* was already a folk tradition by the time it lost the royal patronage of the Malay courts.

The most prominent performances of *zapin* in Sumatra were those given at wedding ceremonies. It was also performed during the ceremonies for *sunatan* (circumcision), *khatam Qur'ān* (completion of learning recitations from the Qur'ān), and *cukur rambut* (shaving of infant's hair). The widespread popularity of the genre with the rites of passage of the Malays of Sumatra is paralleled in the Malay societies of the Riau Archipelago and the Malay Peninsula.

Several assumptions can be made about the spread of *zapin* throughout the Malay world. First, the tradition developed from the influence of Islamic and Arab cultural traditions which may be traced back to the homeland of the Arabs of Hadhramaut. In South-East Asia, *zapin* began to take on a new form and attracted both commoners and aristocrats. The Muslim Malays of the region supported the *zapin* tradition because of its close association with Islamic culture. Being an Arab-derived tradition, *zapin* was accorded high social prestige because the Arabs in South-East Asia were highly regarded for their wealth and their knowledge of Islam.

Secondly, it is very likely that the Malay aristocrats conferred royal recognition and patronage on *Zapin Melayu* when the tradition became more refined; it then enjoyed a higher status than the other Malay dance traditions. Because of the relationship that *zapin* has with Islam and the Arabian Peninsula, it was therefore appropriate for the royal palace to actively promote the tradition through royal patronage. It is also possible that royal patronage was conferred on *zapin* by the Sultans of Malacca. This assumption would help to explain the founding of the *zapin* tradition in the Muar, Pagoh, and Lenga districts of north-west Johore. Since the *zapin* of north-west Johore and Trengganu today are similar to the *zapin* of Penyengat, Siak, and Serdang in East Sumatra, it appears that *zapin* was spread through the intervention of traditional Malay political allegiance and the shifts in the centre of Malay civilization during the formative processes of the Malay sultanates.

Thirdly, even if the power of the Malay monarchs did not play a central role in the spread of the *zapin* tradition throughout the Malay world, the common people themselves may have been the vehicle for the spread of the dance tradition. The need to have *zapin* performances to mark the Malay rites of passage would have ensured the survival of the tradition. The social and political mobility of the Malays contributed to its spread. The Malay commoners transmitted traditions from their places of origin. It is possible that the relatively stable Malay states were centres of Malay culture where traditions such as *zapin* proliferated among the common folk.

The convergence of Malay traders, scholars, mercenary soldiers, and the common folk was dependent on the security provided by stable Malay governments of the day. The Malay Sultans' success in establishing stable political power resulted in the flourishing of trade and commerce as well as new centres of learning. In this process, *zapin* may have attracted the attention of the ruling Sultans and, thus, was performed in the royal palaces. Whether the genre remained an inherent or transient tradition of the Malay royal court, it definitely received sufficient attention from the Malay monarchs. Thus, *zapin* in East Sumatra and Riau was a dance of high social esteem. This would explain the use of highly refined dance techniques which are normally associated with the court. It was imperative that the dancers perform the difficult leg movements in the most subtle and agile manner so that the rugs underneath the dancers remained unruffled.[28]

Whether the spread of the *zapin* tradition along the Straits of Malacca can be historically attributed to the patronage bestowed by the Malay monarchs, or the spread of Islam, or the convergence of the common people in politically stable Malay sultanates, it is clear that *zapin* has transcended political and geographical boundaries along the Straits of Malacca. *Zapin Melayu* is today considered to be a common cultural denominator of the contemporary nation-states of Malaysia, Indonesia, and Singapore.

Zapin and *Alam Melayu*

As a dance and music genre, *zapin* today exists in almost all of maritime South-East Asia, except the Philippines. *Zapin* can be found in areas stretching from Peninsular Malaysia to Indonesia. Although *zapin* is known as a performance tradition of the Islamic Malays, the genre has gained in popularity even among the non-Muslims of Brunei, Indonesia, Malaysia, and Singapore since the middle of the twentieth century. This is largely due to modern means of communication such as the moving pictures of the early cinemas and present-day television transmissions. *Zapin* performances have become visually accessible to the people, either as a fragment of a story in the movies[29] or as a dance performance in television entertainment programmes.[30] Throughout these broad geographic areas the genre may have slightly different names because of dialectal differences in the Malay language,[31] and the performing styles also vary slightly.

The terms used for the dance phrases and the musical accompaniments are similar throughout the different areas. However, this does not mean that the *zapin* tradition has been static or that few changes have occurred in the choreography and musical composition. On the contrary, new choreography has emerged where new ideas have been translated into new dance styles, and new songs have been written to accompany the new *zapin*. Thus, it is common today for *zapin* performers in South-East Asia to perform the moderately different dance styles of the new Malay *zapin*.[32] In Indonesia, the notion of innovational choreography on an existing older tradition is referred to as *kreasi baru* or 'new creation'. In Malaysia, new dance styles choreographed within an older tradition may or may not take a new name. For example, the popular *joget* dance in Malaysia has taken two forms, the old and the new. The former is known as *joget* or *joget lambak* (*joget en masse*) and the latter as *joget moden* (modern *joget*). However, there is a peculiar exception for *zapin* in Malaysia. The contemporary nationally known version is referred to as *zapin* while the older form takes the name *Zapin Melayu* or *Zapin Arab*. The peculiarity of these differences is discussed in subsequent chapters.

However, in spite of *zapin* versatility in adapting new ideas or experimental choreography, the form of the basic elements remains unchanged. These elements ensure the maintenance of the identity of the *zapin* genre. The universal common elements are as follows.

1. A set of musical instruments consisting of: (i) a *gambus* or *'ud*; (ii) several *marwas* hand drums; and (iii) a harmonium or a violin.
2. The music divided into three segments: (i) an improvised free-metred prelude, dominated by the *gambus*, harmonium, or violin; (ii) the interlocking drumming patterns of the *marwas* between musical phrases; and (iii) a coda consisting of interlocking drumming patterns of the *marwas*.
3. The dance divided into three segments: (i) the introductory dance motives; (ii) the dance proper; and (iii) the *tahtim*, *tahto*, or *tahtom* dance phrases, which form the coda to the dance.
4. The basic dance movements: (i) the four-beat dance counts in all the dance phrases; (ii) the bridging of dance sequences by a basic dance phrase and the repeating of dance sequences in the dance proper; and (iii) the *tahtim*, *tahto*, or *tahtom* dance motives are a significantly different form of dance phrase from the rest of the dance movements.

These elements come under the notion of *keseragaman* or uniformity of the *zapin* genre which is congruent with the notion of *keseragaman* or uniformity of the *alam Melayu* (Malay world).

The broad notion of *alam* as a world of people and their environment represents a comprehensive interpretation of the Malay and his world. It is within the *alam Melayu* (Malay world) that the Malays feel united as a *rumpun*, which literally means a clump or a cluster of grass, to which the unity of the Malay world is analogous. It is in this context that *alam Melayu* refers to the Malay people as clustered within a race (*serumpun bangsa*), sharing a similar language (*serumpun bahasa*) and lifestyle. The Malay people express their awareness of their cultural uniformity or *keseragaman* through the sharing of a common identity as well as a similar language and culture.

The *keseragaman* or uniformity is also reflected in the Malay performance traditions, in such aspects as the manner and style of dressing of the performers. All *zapin* performers usually wear a Malay dress known as the *baju melayu* or the *baju teluk belanga*,[33] a pair of trousers (*seluar*, *serawa*, or *sarwa*), a sarong worn over the trousers,[34] and a head covering consisting of a piece of cloth tied round the forehead or a head-dress known as a *songkok* or *peci*.[35] This style of dressing is universal to the Malays in Malaysia, Indonesia, Singapore, and Brunei. The *baju melayu* can be worn as daily attire or can be made more elaborate for ceremonial and official purposes.[36] Thus, *zapin* performers dress in a way that reflects the *keseragaman* (uniformity) of the *alam Melayu* (Malay world).

Another example of Malay universality in *zapin* performance is *zapin* songs, the *pantun* or quatrain form of which is known throughout the Malay world. These are sung either in Malay or in a mixture of Malay and Arabic verses, but usually in the former. The Arabic verses are usually recited as exclamations at the end of a *pantun* stanza or inter-jected between complete quatrains. They give an Arabic and Islamic ambience to the songs and to the *zapin* genre as a whole.

Perhaps the most striking aspect of uniformity or *keseragaman* of the *zapin* performance tradition in respect of the notion of *alam Melayu* is the similarity of the performance elements described earlier. The uniformity of musical instruments, the similarity of *zapin* songs, the universal segmentation of the music and the dance, and the conven-tions in dance movements all reflect a tradition shared by one *rumpun bangsa* (race cluster) in the *alam Melayu*. The *zapin* dance became a tradition of great respectability when it received royal patronage from the Sultans in the various regions of the Malay world. *Zapin* even-tually became a common heritage of the Malays. The uniformity or *keseragaman* in the performance traditions, as in the *zapin*, enables the Malays to express a sense of cultural unity and an awareness of their *alam Melayu*. By displaying common artistic expressions wherever it is found, the *zapin* tradition paves the way for a sense of belonging, not only among small groups such as people of a common dialect or a village, but also among states or nations that make up the wider com-munity of the Malay world, the *alam Melayu*.

1. This information was gathered from the officers at the Department of Education and Culture in Tanjung Pinang and in Pekanbaru.

2. Cultural delegations from the various provinces in Indonesia are often invited to perform in Jakarta. The performance of regional dances and music is considered mandatory. Groups from Medan representing North Sumatra have included *zapin* in their repertoires and are trying to promote it as the regional dance of the province. This has annoyed performers from Riau who believe that *zapin* is rightfully a tradition of the Riau Malays and not of the North Sumatran Malays.

3. Barbara Watson Andaya and Leonard Y. Andaya, *A History of Malaysia* (London: Macmillan Education Ltd., 1987), p. 56.

4. Leonard Y. Andaya, *The Kingdom of Johor 1641–1728* (Kuala Lumpur: Oxford University Press, 1975), p. 23.

5. This was the theory put forward by senior informants in the Lenga and Pagoh areas. There is a general consensus among the performers of *zapin* in these areas that it is quite likely that the Sultan was accompanied by some palace entertainers or followers who were knowledgeable in the art of dancing and the playing of musical instruments.

6. *Sejarah Melayu* is the oldest known chronicle of the Malays of Malacca. It is said to be the finest Malay classic, comparable with the world's finest historical literature.

7. The term Orang Laut is applied to the island and coastal people who inhabit the Riau–Lingga Archipelago, the Pulau Tujuh group, the Batam Archipelago, and the coast

and offshore islands of eastern Sumatra and the southern Malay Peninsula. The relation-ship between the Orang Laut and the rulers of the Malacca–Johore royal family dated from the period of the Srivijaya–Palembang Empire between the seventh and eleventh centuries. This relationship was re-established at the end of the fourteenth century with the founding of the Malacca dynasty (Andaya, op. cit., pp. 44–5).

8. Andaya and Andaya, op. cit., pp. 56–7.

9. Tengku Luckman Sinar (ed.), *Sari Sejarah Serdang 1* (Jakarta: Departemen Pendidikan dan Kebudayaan, Proyek Penerbitan Buku Sastra Indonesia dan Daerah, 1986), p. 39.

10. The Bendahara is an adviser to the Sultan. He may take the office of a finance minister or a treasurer. In the kingdoms of Johore and Malacca, the title Bendahara was traditionally conferred on the principal official of the kingdom.

11. Andaya, op. cit., p. 285.

12. Andaya and Andaya, op. cit., p. 85.

13. Informants from the island of Penyengat believe that the exchanges that took place between the Johore–Riau kingdom and Trengganu after 1718 also involved the sending of a renowned *gamelan* dance teacher, a *nobat* ensemble, and a number of *zapin* performers to Trengganu.

14. The *nobat* ensemble of Trengganu was believed to have been brought over from Penyengat during the rule of Sultan Zainal Abidin III of Trengganu (1881–1918). The *nobat* was borrowed on several occasions by Sultan Zainal Abidin III but was only officially acquired from Penyengat when his son Sultan Muhammad married a daughter of Sultan Abdul Rahman of Riau–Lingga. Together with the *nobat* instruments came the musicians from Riau to Trengganu. (Mubin Sheppard, *Taman Saujana*, Petaling Jaya: International Book Service, 1983, p. 24.) The *nobat* ensemble has been a hallmark of the Malay ruler's legitimacy for over 600 years. It became a treasured possession of Malacca's rulers in 1414. The Sultans of Kedah, Perak, Riau–Johore, and Selangor received their *nobat* from the Malacca lineage. The *nobat* ensemble consists of a single-faced drum called *negara* in Kedah and Patani and *nengkara* in Perak, two barrel-shaped drums called the *gendang*, a silver trumpet of varying length called *nafiri*, and an oboe known as the *serunai*. (Sheppard, op. cit., pp. 17–31; Ku Zam Zam Ku Idris, 'Nobat Diraja Kedah: Warisan Seni Muzik Istana Melayu Melaka', in Abdul Latiff Abu Bakar (ed.), *Warisan Dunia Melayu: Teras Peradaban Malaysia*, Kuala Lumpur: Biro Penerbitan GAPENA, 1985, pp. 174–89.)

15. The Malay *gamelan* of Malaysia originated from Penyengat in Riau. The *gamelan* and several musicians were first brought over to the royal courts of Pahang in 1811 when a marriage between Tun Esah, the sister of Bendahara Tun Ali of Pahang, and Tengku Hussain, the son of Sultan Mahmud Shah III of Riau, was celebrated in Pekan, Pahang. The Malay *gamelan* dance became known as *joget Pahang*. The *gamelan* ensemble remained in the possession of the Pahang royal house until 1915 when it was transferred to the royal house of Trengganu following another royal marriage—Tengku Sulaiman Badrul Alam Shah (the son of Sultan Zainal Abidin III of Trengganu) married Tengku Ampuan Mariam (the daughter of Sultan Ahmad of Pahang) in 1913. Two years later, the Pahang *gamelan* was moved to Trengganu when Cik Zubedah, the mother of Tengku Ampuan Mariam and the third wife of Sultan Ahmad of Pahang, moved with her daughter to Trengganu. Tengku Sulaiman and Tengku Mariam were known to have trained the dancers and musicians of the *gamelan* in Trengganu. When Tengku Sulaiman was crowned Sultan of Trengganu in 1920, former *gamelan* dancers from Pahang were brought over to train Trengganu dancers in the art of *joget gamelan* (Sheppard, op. cit., pp. 1–16; Harun Mat Piah, 'Tradisi Gamelan di Malaysia: Aspek Tradisi dan Pensejarahan, in Harun Mat Piah (ed.), *Gamelan Malaysia*, Kuala Lumpur: Kementerian Kebudayaan, Belia dan Sukan Malaysia, 1983, pp. 13–40).

16. These were the common names cited by informants in Johore, the Riau Islands, and the areas of the former Sultanate of Serdang in Sumatra.

17. Variations in dance sequences are arranged according to selections from several varieties of dance motives clustered under the categories of *alif, pecah, langkah, sut, ayam*

patah, and *tahto*. The following variations are common in the Siak tradition:

Alif variations:
Alip (first letter of the Arabic alphabet)
Alip sembah (homage)
Alif satu (one)
Alif dua (two)
Bunga alif (flower)
Bunga alif pusing satu dan dua (reverse one and two)

Pecah variations:
Pecah lapan pusing satu dan dua (reverse one and two of eight fragmentations)
Pecah ujung (end)
Pecah sepuluh (ten)
Pecah lapan sut (eight)
Pecah dua setengah (two-and-a-half)

Langkah variations:
Langkah satu (one)
Langkah dua (two)
Langkah tiga (three)
Langkah empat (four)
Langkah lima (five)
Langkah enam (six)
Langkah tujuh (seven)
Langkah lapan (eight)

Sut variations:
Sut satu (one)
Sut dua (two)
Sut tiga (three)
Sut empat (four)
Sut manis (sweet)

Ayam variations:
Anak ayam patah (broken chick)
Ayam patah (broken chicken)

Tahto variations:
Minta tahto (request)
Tahto (coda)

See *Laporan Hasil Penyelenggaraan Studi Perbandingan Tari Zapin Se-Daerah Riau* (Pekanbaru, Riau: Proyek Pengembangan Kesenian Riau, 1981).

18. Andaya and Andaya, op. cit., p. 93.

19. H. T. S. Umar Muhammad, Tenas Effendy, and T. Razak Jaafar, *Silsilah Keturunan Raja-Raja Kerajaan Siak Sri Indrapura dan Kerajaan Pelalawan* (Pekanbaru, Riau: Bumi Pustaka, 1988), p. 118.

20. Andaya and Andaya, op. cit., p. 93.

21. Alwi bin Sheikh Alhady, *Malay Customs and Traditions* (Singapore: Donald Moore Press, 1967; repr. New York: AMS Press, 1981), pp. 64–6.

22. Ibid., p. 65.

23. Personal interview with Tengku Luckman Sinar, the son of the late Sultan Sulaiman Shariful Alamshah of Serdang, 19 July 1989.

24. The *mak yong* theatre in Malaysia is thought to have originated from the courts of Patani in what is now southern Thailand. *Mak yong* in Malaysia consists of four leading actresses who play the role of the raja (king), the hero, the queen, and the heroine. They are assisted by a chorus of younger women, male musicians, and comedians. *Mak yong* stories revolve around the magical adventures of a young aristocrat who encounters all forms of challenges. These stories have a happy ending. (Sheppard, op. cit., pp. 33–53.)

25. The performers of the *mak yong* theatre came to Serdang from Patani (Thailand) and Kedah (Malaysia) (Tengku Luckman Sinar (ed.), *Sari Sejarah Serdang 2*, Jakarta: Departemen Pendidikan dan Kebudayaan, Proyek Penerbitan Buku Sastra Indonesia dan Daerah, 1986, p. 30).

26. Ibid.

27. Personal interview with Penghulu Ngah in Perbaungan within the region of the former Serdang Sultanate, 28 July 1989.

28. Informants who had knowledge of the nature of *zapin* performances in the palaces of the Malay Sultans in Riau and East Sumatra explained that the dance floor was always covered with beautiful rugs. It was important for the dancers to ensure that in dancing on these rugs, they did not roll or move the rugs by the impact of their feet. This required them to pay constant attention to the pressure that they put on the supporting leg while twirling, jumping, and skipping. The ruling monarch expected them to achieve this standard whenever *zapin* was performed.

29. Malay movies of the 1950s and 1960s used Malay dances, including *zapin*, for

musical interludes which were interspersed with the development of a plot. For more details, see Chapter 5.

30. *Zapin* has been shown on Malaysian television, Indonesian TVRI, Singapore SBC, and Brunei Television, either as part of a Malay popular entertainment series or as a special series on the traditional performing arts. The former is popular in Malaysia, Singapore, and Brunei, while the latter is more often available in Indonesian television programmes. Special programmes such as the 'Titian Muhibah' (bridge of goodwill), a programme designed for the exchange of cultural programmes between Malaysia and Indonesia, show national and regional dance performances for the viewers of both nations several times a year.

31. The Malay language belongs to the Austronesian stock. The languages of Brunei, Indonesia, Malaysia, Singapore, and the Philippines are of close genetic relationship with one another. The Malay language has a number of regional dialects and the differences between them are mainly phonological. To a certain degree, the dialectal differences are lexical in nature. Grammatical differences are not as common. (See Asmah Haji Omar, *The Malay Peoples of Malaysia and Their Languages*, Kuala Lumpur: Dewan Bahasa dan Pustaka, 1983.) The pronunciation of *zapin* varies depending on the locality. For example, the Malays in Peninsular Malaysia normally name the genre *zapin* or *zapen*, while, the Malays of Sarawak and Kalimantan name it *japen* and the Malays of East Sumatra call it *zapin* or *japin*.

32. New *zapin* choreography must retain all the basic elements or conventions of *zapin* performance such as the types of musical sounds and instruments, the use of a four-beat dance phrase, and the overall segmentation of the piece into three sections.

33. The Malay dress is named after the Johore Malay style of dress which may have originated from Teluk Belanga in Singapore, the former seat of the Johore royal house.

34. A piece of short sarong is worn by rolling and tightening it at the waist. Malay men wear them over their *baju melayu* and trousers. It is commonly known as the *kain sampin*.

35. A Malay cap made of black or blue velvet or cotton fabric.

36. An elaborate *baju melayu* may be made of silk, brocaded fabric, or the expensive gold- and silver-threaded fabric called *songket*. They are worn at weddings and official state functions.

4
Public Entertainment in
the Pre-Second World War Period

By the beginning of the twentieth century, *zapin* had undergone historical and cultural transformations in different areas of the Malay world. In Sumatra and the Riau Islands, *zapin* received aristocratic patronage and the genre was encouraged to expand its repertoire through state-sponsored competitions and palace-related cultural events. *Zapin* performances in the royal palaces became prestigious occasions for the musicians and dancers. Performers invited to dance at the Sultan's palace displayed finesse and reverence, as befits a royal command performance. The Sultan, being the most critical observer, would be pleased with only the finest of dance and musical displays and there was no room for shoddiness or pretension. It was imperative that performers should dance with the utmost precision, grace, and elegance. As long as the Sultans were able to provide moral and economic support for the *zapin* tradition, the enthusiasm for *zapin* remained vibrant and buoyant. The royal patronage of *zapin* in Sumatra lasted until the Second World War.

While *zapin* received aristocratic attention in Sumatra, *zapin* in the Malay Peninsula was never hosted by the Malay Sultans as a palace tradition. In contrast, the tradition remained a rural one, confined to the Malay villages and serving the community whenever there was a need for a public performance. Weddings, circumcision ceremonies, and religious celebrations were the main settings for *zapin* performances. Although lacking royal patronage, the Malay *zapin* genre nevertheless underwent changes by the beginning of the twentieth century which elevated it to a new level of popularity.

By the end of the nineteenth century, the cities of Malacca, Penang, and Singapore (the British Straits Settlements) were the major centres of British colonial economic expansion. These cities rapidly became urbanized, being populated by multi-racial communities of Malays, Chinese, Indians, Punjabis, Eurasians, and others, all of whom were engaged in their respective economic activities. The cities also became the foci for various ethnic theatrical and cultural performances which met the entertainment needs of a cosmopolitan society.

The theatrical medium that had the most significant effect on *zapin*, and eventually lifted it to a new level of creativity and exposed it to a wider public, was the *bangsawan* (Malay opera). The *bangsawan* is a staged musical drama that includes dialogue, songs, music, and dances, of which *zapin* was one. The *bangsawan* theatre became a source of dance choreography and eventually, the village dance tradition of *Zapin Melayu* evolved into a new form in the *bangsawan* theatre.

By the 1930s, the development of urban entertainment parks or amusement parks in Singapore and Penang provided new venues for *zapin* performances. At the commercial dance halls in these parks patrons paid to dance with dance hostesses, known as taxi dancers, whose repertoire ranged from ballroom and Latin dancing to the Malay folk tradition, including *zapin*. The rural male-dominated form of *zapin* gave way to a new form where men and women danced with one another.

Cinemas were introduced in the urban centres of British Malaya in the 1920s and 1930s for the showing of imported films. Films were first produced locally in 1933. The format of Malay films followed that of the *bangsawan* theatre, and dialogue, songs, music, and dances became important elements of films, thus ensuring the success of the fledgeling Malay movie industry. In order to attract Malay audiences, traditional Malay folk dances were included in the movies. The dance repertoires in the movies were largely drawn from the *bangsawan* theatre and the urban entertainment parks, providing Malay dancers with opportunities for new choreography and dance styles.

The *Bangsawan* Theatre

Bangsawan,[1] Malay opera, was the first urban theatre to develop in the Malay Peninsula. Its development was due to the influence of the Persian theatre known as *wayang Parsee*, performances of which started in Penang in the 1870s[2] with the visit of a group of *wayang Parsee* performers from Bombay, India. *Wayang Parsee* had been a popular theatrical form in India in the eighteenth century.[3] Penang, an important British port since its founding in 1786 and a major cosmopolitan centre in South-East Asia with a multi-racial population of Indians, Chinese, Malays, and Europeans, was deemed a suitable place for the promotion of *wayang Parsee*. It was also the home of the mixed-blood Indian–Malays known as Jawi Peranakan.[4] The Jawi Peranakan, who ran successful businesses in Penang, were also familiar with Hindustani stories and songs and, to a certain extent, the Hindustani language.[5] The *wayang Parsee* performers who sang and acted in Hindustani were very well received by the people of Penang. The enactment of stories from India and the Middle East, the sophisticated stage sets, the dazzling costumes, and elaborate musical accompaniments were the major factors for its success in Penang. However, the popularity of *wayang Parsee* declined when the stories and songs remained unchanged. When it eventually collapsed with heavy financial problems in 1885, a local

Indian Muslim businessman by the name of Mamak Pushi bought all the theatre paraphernalia and set up his own theatre company, known as Pushi Indera Bangsawan of Penang.[6] This was the first *bangsawan* group to be established in Penang and was the forerunner of the *bangsawan* groups that emerged at the turn of the century.

The *bangsawan* theatre followed the theatrical concept of the *wayang Parsee* by staging stories which revolved around the lifestyles and romances of the nobility. All the stories had to include songs which passionately conveyed the pathos of being in love, the melancholic grief at losing a loved one, or the sufferings of injustice.[7] The songs were sometimes accompanied by a chorus of dancers dancing around the main actor, the Orang Muda[8] (young man), or the main actress, the Seri Panggung[9] (light of the theatre). The seriousness of the story was occasionally relieved by comedians whose comic roles were woven into the plot of the story. Thus, *bangsawan* had elements of serious drama as well as music and comedy. Songs, music, and dances were inherent to the *bangsawan*.

Another important aspect of the *bangsawan* theatre is the interval between plays. *Bangsawan* was the first Malay theatre genre to use the proscenium stage. Painted backdrops were rolled on to and off the stage. The main stage curtains were opened at the beginning of a play and closed at the end. However, in the intervals between scenes, when backdrops and stage properties were changed, the audience were never left without entertainment. Instead, they were treated to songs and dances independent of the *bangsawan* story. The *bangsawan* theatre intervals were known as extra-turns, an English term which became common usage in *bangsawan*.

Both rising new musicians and dancers and experienced and well-known performers took part in the extra-turns. The extra-turns were as important as the main *bangsawan* drama and musicals in attracting and ensuring continuing patronage of the *bangsawan* theatre. Singers, musicians, comedians, and dancers alternated between the cast of the *bangsawan* proper and the extra-turn performances. The success and popularity of each *bangsawan* troupe depended not only on the excellence of performance of the main drama but also on the quality of the extra-turn performances. Thus the acting and singing abilities of the leading actor and actress, the chorus line, and the supporting actors and actresses, and the work of the technical crew, had to be complemented by outstanding dancing in the extra-turns. It was normal for the prima donnas of the extra-turns to be the main actresses or Seri Panggung of their respective *bangsawan* troupes.

The *bangsawan* musicians performed traditional and popular tunes to accompany the extra-turn songs and dances. Hindustani and Middle Eastern songs were popular with the audience who were also encouraged to make special requests by throwing money on to the stage.[10] This method of requesting songs and dances was popular in the 1920s and 1930s. Some songs were sung to the accompaniment of a chorus line who sang and danced on stage.

Dancers in a *bangsawan* troupe consisted of male and female performers who were trained by the leading dancer. Some of the leading dancers were given special names[11] in recognition of their skills. Minah Yem, known as 'Queen of the Dance', was trained by her mother to dance in the *bangsawan* when she was eight years old. She later became a famous dance teacher of subsequent *bangsawan* dancers. Minah B, another famous dancer and dance teacher in her husband's *bangsawan* troupe, was known as 'Queen Rumba'. She was an expert in Latin dances such as the samba, the mambo, and the rumba.

Dances in the *bangsawan* theatre were often borrowed or derived from existing Malay traditional dances as well as the period's latest dance craze, such as the various Latin dance traditions. Dancers in each *bangsawan* troupe were trained to be versatile in adapting to the numerous dance styles from the various dance traditions in order to stay ahead of other *bangsawan* troupes. The competition between *bangsawan* troupes in embellishing their dance routines even involved the creation of complicated footwork and body movements. The dancers from large *bangsawan* troupes attired themselves in glittering costumes of shining fabrics, gold threads, and sequins.[12]

Malay folk dancing became a professional career for many of the *bangsawan* dancers when more troupes were formed in the 1920s and 1930s. The dancers were recruited from young performers who sought jobs in the *bangsawan* troupes. During that period, it was common for young male teenagers to follow a *bangsawan* troupe and eventually seek permanent jobs with the troupe. They would begin as stage helpers or chorus boys. The more talented ones would be trained as singers and dancers. Later, they became professional dancers with the troupe and learned and practised new dances at specific times during their daily working hours.[13]

Female dancers were more difficult to recruit than male dancers because of the unwillingness of Malay mothers to allow their daughters to become *bangsawan* performers. Female performers had to contend with the social stigma of being considered less refined in character because of their open association with the menfolk in the *bangsawan* troupes. Ordinary Malay women who considered themselves good Muslims and respectable ladies would not even dream of appearing in public in such a manner. It therefore became common practice for troupes to recruit female dancers from among the daughters of *bangsawan* performers. This was one of the reasons that dancing in *bangsawan* troupes became a profession handed down from one generation to the next. However, the development of *bangsawan* dancing as a professional career led to the problem of job-hopping by dancers, who were lured from one troupe to another by better pay and other material inducements.

Malay Dances in the *Bangsawan*

The growing popularity of the *bangsawan* theatre in the 1930s led to the demand for better dance performances. The need for more varied dance repertoires in the *bangsawan* theatre forced dance choreo- graphers to seek new ideas and create new dances to accompany the stories. The dances choreographed for the *bangsawan* play had to add visual impact to the glamour and drama of the *bangsawan* story. Thus, an Arab story had to include elements of the Middle Eastern dance traditions. A common example here is the presentation of belly-dancing in Arab stories. A local legend or history had to include Malay dances which were considered appropriate for a traditional Malay scenario.

However, the dance genres from which *bangsawan* choreographers could cull new ideas were rather limited. There were some ritual- healing dance traditions[14] which were too sacred to serve as dance sources, so the choreographers were left with Malay folk dances to choose from. However, the problem was resolved when the spread of *bangsawan* to other parts of the Peninsula provided dance choreo- graphers with regional folk dance genres from the smaller towns which they could include in their dance repertoires. *Bangsawan* troupes which developed in smaller towns included the Malay Opera of Malacca, the Malay Opera of Selangor, the Norlia Opera of Singapore, the Maha Opera of Muar, the Kinta Opera of Ipoh, and Indera Bongsu of Penang.[15]

The regional Malay folk dance traditions that were introduced into *bangsawan* theatre are very closely related to the pan-Malayan folk dance genres: the *joget, inang, asli,* and *zapin.* The differences between the regional traditions and the pan-Malayan genres are associated with differences in the types of tunes that accompany the dance and with variations in the dance styles. For example, the *canggung* dance, which originated from the northern state of Perlis, is very closely related to the *inang*, while the *cinta sayang* dance from the state of Kedah has a combination of *inang* and *asli* dance styles. The performance of the pan-Malayan folk dance traditions varies from one region to another. The preference by performers from different regions for certain dance styles and specific dance tunes may have contributed to the localization of the pan-Malayan folk dance traditions in their various areas. *Ronggeng, joget lambak,* and *joget moden,* for example, are variants of the *joget* dance tradition, while *mak inang, inang balai,* and *inang deli* are variations of the *inang* dance genre. Throughout the 1930s, the pan- Malayan traditions, the *joget, inang, asli,* and *zapin,* were the basis for traditional dance choreography in the *bangsawan* theatre.

Joget

The *joget*, also referred to as the *ronggeng*, was greatly influenced by Portuguese folk dances. There is a general assumption in Malaysia today that the *joget* was derived from a Portuguese dance known as the *branyo*. However, the scarcity of information on the *branyo* from Malaysian and Portuguese sources in Malaysia suggests that it may have been a mispronunciation of *brundo*. *Brundo* or *branle* was a fifteenth-century court dance which became immensely popular in both the courts and the countryside of the Iberian Peninsula and Italy in the sixteenth century.[16] It could have been brought to the Malay world after 1511 when Malacca fell to the Portuguese.

The main characteristic of *joget* music is the rhythm. It is fast-paced, with duple and triple beat divisions closely related to the European 6/8 dance forms, such as the tarantella and fandango.[17] Characteristics similar to the *joget* are found in the *lagu dua* genre of the Sumatran *ronggeng*. The *joget* is performed by male and female dance partners. They dance around and opposite each other flirtatiously but never touch one another.

Inang

The word *inang* literally means wet nurse.[18] The dance is called *tarian mak inang*, the dance of the wet nurse. The *inang* rhythm consists of a variation of the 4/4 beat pattern which is accented at the end by the gong. The *inang* consists of walking motions either in relatively slow or in fast tempo. A fast-paced *inang* is known as the *masri*.[19] Dancers face one another while making turns and dancing in a circular path around each other. The *inang* was commonly used by *bangsawan* dance choreographers as a base for the creation of dances that used various common objects as dance accessories. The dances thus choreographed were named after the item used in the dance. *Tari piring* (saucer dance), *tari lilin* (candle dance), *tari saputangan* (handkerchief dance), *tari selendang* (shawl dance), and *tari payung* (umbrella dance) became popular in the *bangsawan* theatre where they were used extensively either as dances for the extra-turns or as part of the *bangsawan* story.

Asli

Another Malay folk dance genre which provided the basis for the choreography of *bangsawan* dances is the *asli* dance, the most refined of all Malay folk dance traditions. Hand movements in the *asli* are characterized by the curling and flexing of the fingers while the dancers move in a slow, walking motion. The *asli* song is identified by an eight-beat phrase in 4/4 time. The first four-beat phrase has a fixed pattern while the second four-beat phrase is usually improvised. The fourth and the eighth beats are accented at the end by the gong. The *asli* in the *bangsawan* theatre was usually performed in the extra-turns to accompany singers who sang *asli* tunes. In Sumatra, a musical form similar to the *asli* genre is known as *gunung sayang*. The *gunung sayang* genre is an important element of the *ronggeng*. In Malaysia, however, a variation of the *gunung sayang* is found in the musical traditions of the Malay and Baba[20] communities in Malacca, Penang, and Singapore, where it is known as *dondang sayang* (love lullaby).[21]

Zapin

Zapin, one of the dances commonly performed in Johore and in some parts of the Malay Peninsula, was one of the Malay folk dance traditions that provided the basis for innovations in the *bangsawan* theatre. Although *zapin* was initially known by its village form, the genre became increasingly versatile with new adaptations and creative innovations when it was no longer restricted to male dancers only. The flexibility of having men and women dancing in pairs or in groups on the proscenium stage of the *bangsawan* theatre provided new possibilities in the choreography of *zapin* dances. Dance gestures found in other dances in the *bangsawan* theatre were incorporated within the four-beat *zapin* dance phrase. New dance motives were created to accommodate the changes that were taking place in dance presentations for the extra-turns and in the *bangsawan* stories.

The musical instruments used to accompany the *zapin* dance included the *gambus* (*'ud*), *marwas* hand drums, harmonium, *dok* long drum, and even the Indian *tabla*.[22] (See Chapter 6 for details of the musical instruments.) Some musical instruments, such as the harmonium, the *tabla*, and even the *dok*, were already in use in *wayang Parsee* before they were introduced into the *bangsawan* theatre. Some of the veteran *bangsawan* musicians were former *wayang Parsee* musicians. The *bangsawan* musicians had played *zapin* music on the traditional instruments while performing in *wayang Parsee*. Performing the same music for *bangsawan* was nothing more than continuing an already familiar convention.

As a tradition that was widely believed to have originated from Arab influence on Malay culture, *zapin* was unique. *Bangsawan* dance choreographers drew on *zapin* for the dance repertoire in the religious and Middle Eastern stories enacted by the *bangsawan* troupe. In addition, *zapin* dances were choreographed specifically for the proscenium stage where dancers appeared on and retreated from centre stage through the stage wings, called *sebing*. The multilayered *sebing* in the stage wings enabled the choreographer to create the illusion of dancers appearing from and disappearing into the side walls of the stage.

Another common usage of *zapin* in the *bangsawan* was in the portrayal of dances in the Sultans' courts. The linear formation of *zapin* dancers provided choreographers with the maximum use of space to create the grand dance formations normally associated with court dancing. The stage settings for a Sultan's court in the *bangsawan* theatre closely resembled the actual Balairongseri (Sultan's audience hall) in the palace. The set for the audience hall housed the Sultan's Singgahsana (royal throne) at the far end of the stage. The 'hall' was flanked on both sides by the nobility of the Sultan's court. Dancers performed *zapin* facing their partners in a linear formation, with their backs to the sides of the stage. In this way the dancers avoided presenting their backs to the audience or the actor-Sultan, an action which would have shown a lack of respect and caused embarrassment to the audience. To present or turn one's back to someone while engaging in any form of interpersonal communication is considered rude and uncultured. *Zapin* provided an ideal solution in displaying court dancing in the *bangsawan* theatre without violating Malay etiquette.

The dichotomy between staged dance performances and social dances became evident when the new dance styles from the *bangsawan* theatre spilled over into the urban entertainment parks.

The Urban Entertainment Parks

Urban entertainment parks[23] were the venues for the exploitation of Malay folk dances on a commercial basis. They advocated the spread of the folk dance traditions as a social pastime. The dances in the entertainment parks were performed by patron-dancers who purchased tickets or coupons in order to dance with one or several dance hostesses or taxi dancers. Social dancing between male patrons and female taxi dancers contributed to the development of new styles of performing the Malay folk dances.

Entertainment parks were first established in Singapore in the early 1930s. The three major entertainment parks in Singapore, the Happy World, the Great World, and the New World, were owned by local Chinese investors.[24] Entertainment in the parks ranged from food stalls, *bangsawan* stages, Chinese operas, cinemas, magic shows, gambling stalls, cabarets, to *joget* dance stages—the last two being available in every park. The entertainment parks occupied fairly large tracts of land in order to house all the different forms of public entertainment. They were open in the evenings and attracted large numbers of urban workers. The entertainment parks charged patrons basic entrance fees at the main gates and solicited rental fees from all the stall owners and entertainment companies which provided services in the parks.

The success of the three establishments in Singapore led to the opening of entertainment parks in the Malay Peninsula such as the Fun and Frolic Amusement Park, the Wembley, and the New World in Penang; while Kuala Lumpur had the Great Eastern Ltd., Hollywood Park, and the Bukit Bintang Park; Malacca, the City Park; and Ipoh, the Grand Jubilee Park.

The taxi dancers of the cabarets were known as *penari kabaret* (cabaret dancer), while those of the *pentas joget* (*joget* dance stages) were known as *penari ronggeng* (*ronggeng* dancers). The taxi dancers of both the cabarets and the *pentas joget* were paid fixed monthly salaries by their respective employers, who were known as the *taukeh*.[25] The dancers also received a certain percentage from the sale of dance coupons.[26] The popularity of each dancer on stage determined the amount of money that she earned each night. The taxi dancers worked from 6 p.m. to 8 p.m. and then, after resting for an hour, from 9 p.m. until midnight. Only on special occasions such as Saturday nights and the eve of public holidays did the dancers work until 1 a.m. or 2 a.m. They received some days off and were allowed to rest during the day.

Breakfast and dinner were provided by the *taukeh*, while they purchased their own lunch. The dancers had to buy their own cosmetics and dresses. Being professional dancers, they were expected to be well groomed, to dress beautifully, and to wear attractive facial make-up.

Katherine Sim, the wife of a British expatriate, described the appearance of the *ronggeng* dancers:

The four dancing girls, their full lips scarlet, their faces pale powdered masks and their eyes enormous with kohl were already doing the first slow steps of the dance. They each wore long heavy silk jackets fitting to the waist and outlining the hips, over flowered sarongs; gold necklaces over their high stiff collars and gold anklets round their bare ankles. Their black hair was done in a large knot at the back of the head, encircled with heavily scented white flowers, while each wore a single pink flower tucked coquettishly behind one ear. The colours of their clothes were apple green, magenta pink and orange.[27]

In spite of their appearance on stage and their willingness to dance with any men who had purchased coupons, the taxi dancers on the *joget* stages were forbidden to touch or be touched by their patron-dancers:

The girls must not be touched, the men can only follow their steps while the monotonous music gets faster and faster working up to a terrific crescendo. Curiously, inspite of the mounting speed there was nothing abandoned about it. Most of the girls danced with a pretence of aloofness and boredom. They were of course, all professional dancers, hired for the evening as one would hire a cabaret show, and of a low class.[28]

The ethics of Malay folk dancing were upheld by the avoidance of body contact between men and women. The holding of hands, permissible in Western ballroom dancing, was considered improper. The *ronggeng* dancers and the patron-dancers were, however, allowed to dance close to one another. Thus, it was common practice for the patron-dancers to dance around their partners or flirtatiously move back and forth with them in a weaving pattern:

The steps of the Ronggeng dancer are little more than a rhythmic shuffle which becomes more difficult and intricate as the music grows faster. There is a system of 'cutting out' the men which gives an appearance of the girls' line weaving through the men's line, each always taking great care not to touch the other.[29]

Naturally, the dance stage also served as the appropriate place for the patron-dancers to carry on long conversations with their favourite partners, so they usually purchased wads of coupons to enable them to dance several rounds together, uninterrupted by other patron-dancers.

The only exceptions to the dance conventions described above were found in the cabarets and dance halls of the entertainment parks. These places were more sophisticated than the open-air *joget* dance stages in terms of building structure, musical orchestrations,[30] and the dance repertoires offered by their taxi dancers. Apart from the *ronggeng* dances, their repertoire also included some form of Western ballroom dancing, introduced to satisfy the requirements of their patron-dancers. Whereas the patrons of the *joget* dance stages were largely blue-collar workers, the cabarets and dance halls were frequented by white-collar workers and wealthier patrons. The fees, slightly higher than those of the *joget* dance stages, were commensurate with repertoires that permitted patron-dancers to engage in bodily contact such as holding the hands and the hips of the taxi dancers. Dances like the waltz, the fox-trot, the tango, and the quickstep were popular in these establishments.

Although the *ronggeng* dancers of the *joget* dance stages were not required to know Western ballroom dances, they were nevertheless taught a wide range of dances by the group's leading dancer or by their dance teachers. In most cases, the teacher was the wife of the group's *taukeh*.[31] The taxi dancers were expected to perform dances from the Western Latin tradition, such as the samba, the mambo, the rumba, and the cha-cha, as well as all the Malay folk dances. As in the *bangsawan* theatre, the Malay folk dances were identified under the four major genres: the *joget*, *inang*, *asli*, and *zapin*. In the 1930s, however, it was also common to identify all four pan-Malayan Malay folk dances as the *ronggeng* dances,[32] because of the grace and ease with which the *ronggeng* dancers were able to dance them.

The establishment of *pentas joget* (*joget* dance stages), cabarets, and dance halls and the employment of taxi dancers in these establishments in the urban entertainment parks not only facilitated public dancing but also established new trends of performing the Malay folk dance traditions. Like the *bangsawan* theatre, the entertainment parks were instrumental in the spread of these traditions throughout the Malay Peninsula. Likewise, the array of repertoires promoted by the entertainment parks inspired *bangsawan* dance choreographers to more creative work. Perhaps the biggest challenge to Malay folk dances posed by the entertainment parks was the competition from the introduction of Western dance crazes. The survival of these folk dances depended very much on the support of the patron-dancers. The popularity of the dances was indicated by the frequency with which patron-dancers requested them. Malay folk dances were no longer performed in the manner of village performances. Taxi dancers and their teachers created new dance formations with new motives and styles in order to ensure continued interest from patron-dancers. Dance motives were adapted from other dance traditions. Even basic movements of Latin dance traditions were incorporated into the Malay traditions. Traces of the rumba, the mambo, and the cha-cha were successfully incorporated into the *joget*, *inang*, and *zapin*. The new motives created in the Malay folk dances posed new challenges to the patron-dancers and those which became popular with them were eventually accepted as part of the larger repertoire of the *ronggeng*.

The promotion of new dance styles in the urban entertainment parks had a lasting effect on the Malay folk dance traditions. In the case of *zapin*, the introduction of new dance motives in the *bangsawan* theatre and on the *pentas joget* not only changed the dance from a village to an urban tradition, but also provided the inspiration for choreographers to create variations which highlighted the versatility of performers. It meant that *zapin* could be performed by as few as two dancers instead of the rows of male dancers of the traditional village formation. The new style enabled a pair of dancers to dance in any corner of the dance stage, just as in other social dances. *Zapin* became a one-to-one dance phenomenon instead of the traditional group-to-group dance.

Patron-dancers had to learn the new and sometimes complex dance motives, either by watching the taxi dancers or by learning from friends who frequented the commercial dance stages in the entertainment parks. Folk dancing in the entertainment parks became more challenging and thus was further removed from the village version. The new *zapin* dance that was eventually to become a national tradition would also finally displace village *Zapin Melayu*. The *bangsawan*, the urban entertainment parks, and then the Malay movie industry were the catalysts for the spread of the new *zapin* tradition.

The Development of the Malay Movie Industry

Prior to the birth of the Malay movie industry in 1933 movies from America, India, the Middle East, and China were shown in Malaya and Singapore.[33] In the 1920s and 1930s, permanent cinemas were built in major towns and cities to cater to the popular demand for the screening of foreign movies. There were also mobile cinemas, which were set up in fields or rented buildings.

Hindustani movies imported from India were very popular with the Malays, Indians, and the Jawi Peranakan in the 1930s, probably because of their familiar themes and the admixture of songs, music, and dances which gave them a resemblance to the *wayang Parsee* and later the *bangsawan* theatre. Equally popular were the Arab movies imported from Egypt and Beirut, Lebanon. The Arab movies that laid much emphasis on religious and nationalist themes were popular with the Malays and other Muslims. Arab songs in movies also attracted much public attention.

The first Malay films shown in Malaya and Singapore in the early 1930s were not produced locally but were imported from Indonesia. Although feature films were first produced in Indonesia in 1926, the first being *Loetoeng Kasaroeng* (The Astray Monkey), which was produced by G. Kruger,[34] the importation of Indonesian movies into Malaya and Singapore only began in 1932.[35] The first films imported were entitled *Kahwin Paksa* (Forced Marriage), *Njai Dasima* (The Story of Njai Dasima), and *Semangat Ular* (Forces of the Snake).[36] Indonesian movies were popular because they resembled the *bangsawan* format known as *stambul*[37] in Indonesian. Another important aspect of the Indonesian movies that proved popular with the audiences was the *keroncong* songs.[38]

Inspired by the success of the Indonesian films in Malaya and Singapore, the first Malay film company was formed in Singapore by

Motilal Chemical Company of India in 1933. The company was headed by Mr Chisty, who became the company's film producer.[39] An Indian film director, B. S. Rajhan, was appointed their film director in Singapore. The first film produced by the company was an Arab romance entitled *Laila Majnun*, which made use of songs and dances from Egypt. The cast was recruited from the *bangsawan* theatre.

In 1938, Runme Run Shaw, a rich Chinese entrepreneur started Shaw Brothers Company at a site on Jalan Ampas (Ampas Road) in Singapore. Although Shaw Brothers was more successful in film-making after the Second World War, the company managed to produce several films between 1939 and 1941. The films produced during these years were *Mutiara* (Pearl), *Bermadu* (Polygamy), *Topeng Syaitan* (Satan's Mask), and *Hancur Hati* (Broken Hearted). Since Shaw Brothers was interested in making profits from all its financial investments in Malay movies, the films produced included all elements of entertainment popular during the period.

Like Motilal Chemical Company, Shaw Brothers recruited *bangsawan* actors and actresses, dancers, musicians, singers, and comedians as cast members. This not only ensured the availability of a capable cast but also took advantage of the fame of some of the successful *bangsawan* actors. The musicians who were already playing for the *bangsawan* and the *pentas joget* as well as in the cabarets needed almost no further training to play the music for Malay movies. The dancers who were hired from the same establishments were also already accomplished professional dancers and had only to learn to adjust to the requirements of film-making in order to ensure a smooth transition from stage to studio dancing.[40]

The Malay movies produced before the Second World War contained all the elements of the *bangsawan* theatre tradition—music, dances, songs, dialogue, and comedy—except extra-turns. Extra-turns were not required in film-making since it was not necessary to provide entertainment during set changes. These took place outside the film shooting schedules and did not occur between scenes as in the *bangsawan* theatre. Dances from the extra-turns, however, were incorporated into movies as part of the song-and-dance sequences. The inclusion of songs and dances between pieces of dialogue in the Malay movies was due to the influence of Hindustani movies.

The production of Malay movies—and, in particular, film-making techniques themselves—had a significant impact on the promotion of Malay folk dances, both before, and more so after, the Second World War. The cutting and editing of dance scenes in film-making required producers to use many different camera angles to produce multi-perspective shots of dance performances during songs. The result of splicing the different perspectives of the same dance repertoire was a collage of dance motives which dazzled movie-goers. The fascination with Malay dances in the early years of Malay film-making (1933–41) laid the foundations for a growing awareness in Malay society of the versatility of *joget*, *inang*, *asli*, and *zapin*.

Like the other Malay folk dance traditions, *zapin* served the commercial purposes of the Malay movie industry. The complex *zapin* footwork and dance motives that developed in the *bangsawan* and the urban entertainment parks began to reach other regions in Malaya through the Malay movies. The new *zapin* dance styles and dance motives which became popular with movie-goers were even imitated on the *pentas joget* and in cabarets.

The popularity of Latin dance traditions and, to some extent, the ballroom dance tradition went beyond the dance halls and cabarets when these dances became the sources for the creation of new *zapin* dance motives. The cha-cha, the mambo, the samba, and the tango from the Latin repertoire and the waltzes and foxtrots from the ballroom tradition were sources of inspiration in the creation of new *zapin* dance motives. New *zapin* repertoires had commercial value because of the demand for *zapin* in the Malay movie industry. Furthermore, the extra-turns in the *bangsawan* theatre needed new styles to attract patrons. The introduction of the new style of *zapin* in the theatre and the movies popularized *zapin* as a dance to be performed by *ronggeng* girls and taxi dancers on the mobile *pentas joget* as well as in the dance halls. Ironically, *zapin* eventually became a popular dance genre in the dance halls from which the tradition had earlier been borrowed.

Although the Malay movie industry virtually ceased production during the Second World War, it nevertheless enabled *zapin* and other Malay folk dance traditions to acquire greater public recognition. With the revival of the industry after the war, the new *zapin* was poised to replace village *zapin*, relegating it to a position as a localized tradition that would never achieve national status.

1. The word *bangsawan* consists of two words, *bangsa* and *wan*. *Bangsa* refers to a race, ethnic group, or specific group of people, while *wan* is the name or title ascribed to members of Malay aristocratic families. *Bangsawan*, therefore, refers to a group of people from the aristocratic families (Rahmah Bujang, *Sejarah Perkembangan Drama Bangsawan di Tanah Melayu dan Singapura*, Kuala Lumpur: Dewan Bahasa dan Pustaka, Kementerian Pelajaran Malaysia, 1975, p. 20). Additional information on the origin of the word is found in Wan Abdul Kadir's description of the *bangsawan* theatre. It was noted that the group of people who first established the *bangsawan* theatre in Penang came from the Wan family. They were Wan Tamby S'ah, Wan Maidin, Wan Mat Kapri, Wan Pilus, Wan Nyian, and Pak Wan Long. They named their group the 'Wan people' or '*bangsawan*'. (Wan Abdul Kadir, *Budaya Popular dalam Masyarakat Melayu Bandaran*, Kuala Lumpur: Dewan Bahasa dan Pustaka, Kementerian Pendidikan Malaysia, 1988, p. 38; Tunku Abdul Rahman, *As a Matter of Interest*, Kuala Lumpur: Heinemann Educational Books (Asia), 1982, pp. 236–41.)

2. The *wayang Parsee* troupe consisted of men and women who performed legendary stories from India and the Middle East. They acted and sang in Hindustani. (Ghulam Sarwar Yousof, 'Bangsawan: Opera Melayu (Bahagian Pertama)', *Dewan Budaya*, November 1986, p. 52.)

3. Ghulam Sarwar Yousof, 'Bangsawan: The People's Opera', *Pulau Pinang*, January–February 1989.

4. Jawi Peranakan refers to the offspring of the inter-racial marriages between Indian and Malay parents. They speak a dialect of the Malay language known as Jawi Pekan. For more details on the Jawi Peranakan, see Judith A. Nagata, 'What Is a Malay? Situational Selection of Ethnic Identity in a Plural Society', *American Ethnologist*, Vol. 2, No. 2 (1974) and Mohd Aris Haji Othman, *Identiti Etnik Melayu*, Petaling Jaya: Penerbit Fajar Bakti, 1985.

5. Hindustani, a hybrid of Hindi (an Indo–Aryan language) and Farsi (Persian language), has been used in northern India since the thirteenth century. It is spoken today in various parts of India. ('India', *The New Encyclopaedia Britannica*, 15th edn., Vol. 21, 1987.)

6. The words *indera* and *bangsawan* both refer to the social status of persons with aristocratic backgrounds. The word *indera bangsawan* was used by Mamak Pushi to refer to the high social background of his *bangsawan* performers. He deliberately used the name to lure real aristocrats to join his *bangsawan* theatre. Unfortunately, his plan failed because none of his *bangsawan* performers was from an aristocratic family. (Rahmah Bujang, op. cit., p. 22.)

7. Ibid., p. 53. Popular themes portrayed in the *bangsawan* stories varied. Some stories depicted the cruelty of kings against subjects, of stepmothers against stepchildren, and that of a king's young wife towards the senior wife in a polygamous marriage. Love stories were also common. Some of them were centred on the love and sufferings of lovers of different social status, and between mythical characters of the Malay legends.

8. The Orang Muda must be good looking, a good singer, and an excellent actor, and should be well built. Famous Orang Muda received high salaries and enjoyed better living conditions than the regular male *bangsawan* performers.

9. The *bangsawan* prima donna was known as the Seri Panggung and was required to be pretty, to be fair in complexion, to have an excellent voice, and to be a good actress and dancer. Like the Orang Muda, the Seri Panggung was well paid and lived more comfortably than the regular female *bangsawan* performers.

10. Normally, the money was wrapped in a piece of paper on which was written the song requested. It was thrown at the feet of the singer who would oblige by singing the song requested. The money was for the singer to keep.

11. The names or titles were in English. It was considered prestigious for *bangsawan* performers to be given titles in the English language. This can perhaps be attributed to the pervasive colonial mentality in Malaya and Singapore during the British period.

12. Before electricity became available in the *bangsawan* theatre, gas lamps were used to illuminate the stage. The flickering lights and the glow of the gas lamps reflected off the shining fabrics created dazzling effects. (Rahmah Bujang, op. cit., pp. 111–15.)

13. Some hours were reserved during the day for dance practices. Dancers rehearsed old and new dances within the *bangsawan* living quarters. The rehearsals were important in order to ensure complete familiarity with the dance repertoires. Dances in the extra-turns varied from one night to the next.

14. Ritual-healing dance traditions such as the *main puteri*, *tari balai*, and *tari belian* involved incantations of ritual formulas known only to the shaman or spirit mediums (the *bomoh*, *pawang*, or Tok Mindok). The dance repertoire served as a link between the human world and the spirit world. It was considered harmful to perform these dances without the presence of the *pawang* or the shaman.

15. For more details on the locations of the *bangsawan* troupes in Malaya and Singapore, see Rahmah Bujang, op. cit., pp. 28–30.

16. The *brundo* or *branle* was typically danced in the form of a ring which might change into a file advancing sideways. The *branle* double and *branle* simple were in duple metre whereas the *branle gai* was in triple metre. The descendants of early Portuguese settlers in Malacca still perform dances similar to the *brundo* or *branle* today. For information on the *brundo* or *branle*, refer to *Grove's Dictionary of Music and Musicians*, Vol. 1, London: Macmillan, 1954, pp. 910–11; *Harvard Dictionary of Music*, 2nd edn., Cambridge, Massachusetts: The Belknap Press of Harvard University Press, 1969, p. 105; and W. G. Raffee, *Dictionary of the Dance*, New York: A. S. Barnes and Company, 1975, p. 77.

17. The fandango is a dance in quick 3/4 or 6/8 time performed by a pair of dancers and is extremely popular in Andalusia and the Basque provinces in Spain. The fandango is accompanied by guitars and castanets, alternating with sung couplets. The tarantella is a courting dance of South Italy, Sicily, and Sardinia. The music is in 3/8 or 6/8 time which gradually increases in speed. The tarantella is usually danced by a man and a woman to the accompaniment of mandolins, guitars, and a drum. (Raffee, op. cit., pp. 175 and 493.)

18. The word *mak* is a truncation and also a familiar or diminutive form of the word *emak* which means mother. The term *mak inang* refers to the lady-like qualities of the women dancers which are likened to the graceful movements of the wet nurses.

19. James D. Chopyak, 'Music in Modern Malaysia: A Survey of the Musics Affecting the Development of Malaysian Popular Music', *Asian Music*, 18 (1), pp. 120–1.

20. The terms Baba and Nyonya are used in reference to the Chinese (or their parents) who were born in Penang, Malacca, and Singapore during British rule. They were also known as Straits-born Chinese, obviously referring to the British Straits Settlements. The Baba (male) and Nyonya (female) speak Malay as a home language and have incorporated Chinese and Malay cultural traditions into their lifestyle.

21. *Dondang Sayang* is a traditional Malay art of singing which uses the Malay *pantun* (quatrain) as a poetic form. Utilizing an eight-beat phrase in 4/4 time as in the *asli* tradition, the singers alternate singing the *pantun*. For information on *dondang sayang*, see Philip L. Thomas, *Like Tigers Around a Piece of Meat: The Baba Style of Dondang Sayang*, Singapore: Institute of Southeast Asian Studies, 1986.

22. The *tabla* is a drum from north India. It is played together with another drum known as the *baya*. Both are kettle-shaped. The *tabla* is played with the right hand and the *baya* with the left hand. Both drums have tuning patches on the drum heads. (William P. Malm, *Music Cultures of the Pacific, the Near East, and Asia*, New Jersey: Prentice Hall, 1967, p. 77.)

23. The term 'entertainment park' is used instead of 'amusement park' because it is a closer translation of *taman hiburan*, the Malay term used to refer to the venue in which social and entertainment facilities were made available to the public. *Taman* refers to park or garden, and *hiburan* refers to entertainment.

24. The Chinese entrepreneurs in Singapore were the first to realize the economic potential in investing in public services. The expansion of the colonial economy brought about a migration of rural labourers into major cities and towns, and they represented an untapped source of revenue in night-time entertainment. The success of Singapore's entertainment parks led local Chinese investors to open similar parks in other towns and cities in Malaya.

25. The *taukeh* were responsible for all the financial expenses required to keep the dancers together. They also paid medical expenses and to some extent paid for the supply of beauty aids to the dancers, repairs to the musical instruments, and even the musicians' attire.

26. In the 1930s, dance coupons or tickets were sold at the price of four for one Straits dollar for night performances and six for one Straits dollar for evening performances. The taxi dancers received thirteen cents (in Straits currency) for each ticket. (Wan Abdul Kadir, *Budaya Popular*, pp. 133–4.)

27. Katherine Sim, *Malayan Landscape*, London: Michael Joseph, 1946, p. 52.

28. Ibid.

29. Ibid., p. 53.

30. The *joget* dancers and musicians were also hired for weddings and other social functions held outside the entertainment parks. Because of the need for mobility, the *joget* groups had fewer musicians and their musical instruments were lighter and less sophisticated. In contrast, cabaret and dance hall performers were more permanently tied to their performance locations. They played in bigger ensembles and their musical instruments were more varied.

31. It was common practice for the leading dancers and musicians in *ronggeng* groups to marry one another and set up a new group. The husband would be the *taukeh* and his wife the dance instructor. Since the success of these groups depended on good dancers

and musicians, the husband-and-wife team would use their experiences as guidelines for the running of their own team of performers. (Personal interviews with Pak Malim Othman, the *taukeh* of Orkes Aslirama of Singapore, July 1989 and with Pak Hashim Haji Shukor, a former *taukeh* of a *ronggeng* group in Muar, August 1989.)

32. The *ronggeng* tradition of Malaya and Singapore was quite different from that of Sumatra. The Sumatran *ronggeng*, which exists to the present day, consists of five different musical sections: the *gunung sayang*, *lagu dua*, *inang*, *zapin*, and a section called *patam-patam*. In contrast, the *ronggeng* of Malaya and Singapore consisted of a mixture of two genres, the *joget* and *inang*. *Pantun* exchanges between the *ronggeng* singers and the patron-dancers, which were dominant in the Sumatran *ronggeng*, were of lesser importance in the Malayan and Singapore *ronggeng*.

33. Wan Abdul Kadir, *Budaya Popular*, pp. 146–50.

34. *Indonesian Film Catalogue*, Jakarta: National Film Council of Indonesia, 1982, p. 62.

35. Ibid. Prior to 1932, Indonesian feature films produced by the Dutch and Chinese were of poor quality and therefore unable to compete with other foreign films already in circulation in Malaya and Singapore. The Dutch film producers had to cease operations in Indonesia when the films produced were barely able to recover the investments.

36. Wan Abdul Kadir, *Budaya Popular*, pp. 173–5.

37. *Stambul* was the name of the *bangsawan* theatre that was first established in Batavia (Jakarta), Indonesia. The *Stambul* theatre was named after the financier Jaafar Turki (Jaafar the Turk), who had bought Pushi Indera Bangsawan from Mohammad Pushi when it fell into financial difficulties. Pushi Indera Bangsawan had come to Batavia after successful tours of Malaya and Singapore. Ironically, Batavia became its last and final stop. The new theatre under the leadership of Jaafar Turki performed Middle Eastern stories. *Stambul* was derived from Istanbul, the capital of Turkey, which was considered a prestigious centre of learning and culture. (Rahmah Bujang, op. cit., pp. 22–3.)

38. The *keroncong* genre in Malaysia and Indonesia is believed to have been influenced by the Portuguese after the sixteenth century. In Malaysia, the *keroncong* ensemble is known as *orkes keroncong* (*keroncong* orchestra). The ensemble consists of musicians who play the guitar, violin, ukelele, double bass, steel guitar, flute, and drums. The songs are of the sentimental variety and are sung by female vocalists. (See Judith Becker, 'Kroncong, Indonesian Popular Music', *Asian Music*, 7 (1), pp. 14–18.; Heins Ernst, 'Kroncong and Tanjidor: Two Cases of Urban Folk Music in Jakarta', *Asian Music*, 7 (1), pp. 20–32; and Ariff Ahmad, *Seni Musik Keroncong*, Kuala Lumpur: Pusat Kebudayaan Universiti Malaya, 1980.)

39. Wan Abdul Kadir, *Budaya Popular*, p. 181 and Jamil Sulong, 'Aperçu Sur L'Histoire Du Cinema Malais', *Archipel*, 5 (1973), pp. 231–5.

40. Personal interview with Dato L. Krishnan of Gaya Film, August 1989.

5
The Malay Movie Industry in the 1950s

THE end of the Second World War marked a new beginning for the entertainment industries in Malaya and Singapore. The British colonial government which returned to Malaya and Singapore after the war commenced a programme of rehabilitating the economy and rebuilding the country's infrastructure. Cities and towns were revived in their former role as political, economic, and administrative centres. The peoples of Malaya and Singapore were encouraged to pursue their normal livelihoods. The Malayan Civil Service was reinstated, while businesses and free enterprise were encouraged anew. Urban dwellers who had fled to the countryside during the war years of 1941–5 began to return to the urban labour force. Public entertainment was also revitalized.

The 1950s was an important period for the development of Malay folk dances. The creation of new dance repertoires and styles based on Malay folk dance traditions was stimulated by the increase in the demand for Malay dances in the Malay movie industry and the entertainment parks. Places of public entertainment, including the *bangsawan* theatres, the urban entertainment parks housing the *joget* or *ronggeng* dance stages and the cabarets, and the Malay movies reopened. Larger and more attractive theatres and dance halls were built, either within the urban entertainment parks or as separate entities. As more cabarets and night-clubs were built to cater to the growing urban population, more dancers, singers, and musicians were employed. Former *bangsawan* performers, taxi dancers, singers, and movie actors and actresses began to return to their professions. The remuneration of performers was better than in the period before the war, mainly because of the social benefits provided either by the proprietors or by the *taukeh*. The most prestigious business in the entertainment world at that time was the Malay movie industry.

The 1950s and 1960s also saw an abundance of popular periodicals which catered to the followers of movies, other public entertainment, and fashion.[1] Movie stars and singers became the focus of the news media. The high fashion and style of the Malay movie stars and popular singers were quickly imitated by the public. Songs and dances in the Malay movies were repeated in school concerts and talent shows all over the country. New dance crazes which developed at the night spots of the bigger cities such as Singapore, Kuala Lumpur, and Penang became popular with the public. This was the period when the new *zapin* became nationally known and performed throughout Malaya and Singapore.

The new *zapin* was very different from the *Zapin Melayu* or village *zapin*. The performance styles of the new *zapin* were copied from those found on the *joget* dance stages and in the cabarets and Malay movies. The concept of stage dancing became an integral part of the new *zapin* performances; *zapin* dances were choreographed for the proscenium stage. The dancers were trained to understand the importance of proper stage appearance, which included uniformity in dance attire, stage make-up, precision in dance movements, and ensuring that dancers did not turn their backs to the audience—*zapin* dances were always performed with the dancers' fronts or side profiles towards the audience. This was not only in accordance with the convention of stage dancing in the *bangsawan* theatre, but also in compliance with the social decorum of dancing on elevated, closed, picture-framed proscenium stages. The numerous constraints imposed upon the dancers by virtue of dancing on a proscenium stage influenced *zapin* dance choreography as *zapin* dances were choreographed solely for stage performance. The traditional venue for the *Zapin Melayu*, open spaces or the wooden floors of Malay houses became a thing of the past, as did the traditional in-the-round or linear formation. The interaction between dancers and audience that occurred in traditional village performances of *Zapin Melayu* were no longer possible when the dancers and the audience were physically separated by the proscenium stage.

The Early Post-war Years

The first film company to commence production after the Second World War was Malay Film Arts Production, its first Malay movie being entitled *Seruan Merdeka* (Call for Independence), which was directed by B. S. Rajhan.[2] However, this commercial venture ended abruptly in 1947 because of the lack of cinemas. All the cinemas in working condition after the war were owned and operated by Shaw Brothers Company, which also owned the three major entertainment parks in Singapore[3] and several others in Malaya and was about to become a major entertainment conglomerate. Their first financial success in Malay movies came with the screening of *Chempaka* (The Frangipani, a sweet-smelling tropical flower). It was after this success that Shaw Brothers established a permanent company, Malay Film Production (MFP), to produce other Malay movies. In 1949, MFP produced three highly successful movies, *Noor Asmara* (Light of Romance), *Nilam* (Sapphire), and *Nasib* (Luck or Fortune). These movies were directed by B. S. Rajhan and starred S. Roomai Noor and Kasma Booty.[4]

The success of these Malay movies encouraged other entrepreneurs to set up movie companies. One, Nusantara Film Productions, was short-lived, and had to stop production because of the lack of cinemas that would screen its movies. Another, Cathay Kris Film Production, was set up in 1951 by two Chinese entrepreneurs, Ho Ah Loke and Loke Wan Tho. Ho, who also owned Rimau Film Production, and Loke, the millionaire owner of Cathay Company, already owned cinemas in almost all the big towns in Malaya and Singapore.[5] Cathay Kris went into full operation at the East Coast Road studio in Singapore. By 1952, Shaw Brothers' MFP and Cathay Kris were the only film companies in Singapore that were financially successful. They had a monopoly over Malay movie production in Malaya and Singapore.

To ensure continuous success in the production of Malay movies, MFP and Cathay Kris recruited film directors from India and even the Philippines, not being willing to gamble on training Malays as film directors. Almost all their technical crews were recruited from Hong Kong.

Indian Movie-making Techniques

Indian movie directors who made Malay movies in Singapore, such as B. S. Rajhan, B. N. Rau, Phani Majumdar, L. Krishnan, V. Girimajy, Diresh Gosh, S. Ramanathan, and K. R. S. Sastry were all familiar with the techniques and performance styles of movie-making in India,[6] and utilized these when making Malay movies. Successful Indian movies produced in Bombay, Calcutta, and Madras in the 1950s followed a prescribed formula.

The formula as dictated by exhibitor and distributor [of films], called for one or two major stars, at least half a dozen songs, and a few dances. The story was of declining importance. It was conceived and developed toward one objective: exploitation of the idolized star. The subject matter, with increasing concentration, was romance. An overwhelming number of Bombay films now began with the chance acquaintance of hero and heroine, often in unconventional manner and novel setting. In backgrounds and characters there was strong bias toward the glamorous. Obstacles were usually provided by villainy or accident, not by social problems. Dance and song provided conventionalized substitutes for love-making and emotional crisis.[7]

Like the *bangsawan* theatre, Malay movies used famous stars to attract the audience. The heroes and heroines of Malay movies were largely responsible for the success of the films. The idolization of actors and actresses by the public was exploited by film producers and movie directors to gain maximum economic success. Movie idols such as P. Ramlee, Ahmad Mahmood, Haji Mahdi, and S. Roomai Noor were teamed with equally famous and glamorous actresses such as Kasma Booty, Rokiah Jaafar, Mariam Rahim, Maria Menado, Saadiah, Neng Yatimah, Rosnani, and Latifah Omar who became popular movie stars by virtue of their personal beauty and acting talents.[8]

Malay movie stories were adapted from stories in Hindustani movies and from the *bangsawan* theatre.[9] As in Indian movies, the stories centred on the romance between the hero and the heroine, whose coming together was impeded by all forms of social obstacles, such as differences in social class and economic status.

Although Indian movie directors were able to provide local film companies with the formula for successful Malay movie productions, they had other problems to overcome. Their lack of familiarity with the socio-cultural background of the Malays made it difficult for them to fully integrate Malay culture into the movies.[10] The scripts for Malay movies produced in the early 1950s were often poor: words and sentences which were transposed from the *bangsawan* theatre became stiff and rigid when spoken on screen. There were common mistakes in language usage due to the inability of Indian movie directors to supervise scriptwriting. This problem, however, was solved in the late 1950s when more capable scriptwriters and indigenous actors were appointed as movie directors. Among the successful Malay movie directors were P. Ramlee, who directed *Penarik Beca* (Trishaw Peddler) in 1955 for Shaw Brothers,[11] S. Roomai Noor, who directed *Adam* (Adam) for Cathay Kris in 1957, and Jamil Sulong, who did *Batu Belah Batu Bertangkup* (The Split-and-Shut Rock) in 1958.[12]

The Indian movie directors and, to a certain extent, their Malay counterparts preferred to leave the songwriting and choreography to the resident and part-time composers and choreographers. With the exception of P. Ramlee,[13] who became one of the best and most popular Malay composers, other movie directors relied on musicians and composers who played in urban entertainment parks and *joget* dance stages in Singapore. Composers and musicians such as Zubir Ismail, Osman Ahmad, and Yusuf B. became major songwriters and composers for the Malay movie industry.

Dances in the Malay movies were adapted from the extra-turns of the *bangsawan* theatre and from the popular dances in the entertainment parks. Former *bangsawan* dancers were employed by the film companies as resident dancers and choreographers. The Malay movie directors, with the exception of P. Ramlee who himself helped in dance choreography,[14] depended on the dancers and dance instructors from the *bangsawan* theatres, the *ronggeng* or *joget* dance stages, and the cabarets either in the entertainment parks or outside them. According to Dato L. Krishnan, who was one of the pioneering Indian movie directors employed in Singapore, Indian movie directors were ignorant of the kind of indigenous dances that should be included in each movie. The most that the movie directors were able to do was to tell the dance instructors and choreographers of the background against which the dances would be performed. Some were for palace scenes while others were for village festivities which were often performed in front of the *penghulu* or headman's house. Although the movie directors had high expectations of the dancers, they were seldom disappointed, since most of the dancers and choreographers were keen to perform to the best of their ability in order to be in the movies. This was primarily because the Malay movie would seem more glamorous than the world of live performances on dance and *bangsawan* stages. It can also be attributed to the decline in the popularity of the *bangsawan* theatre, as a result of which most of its star actors and actresses, dancers, and musicians were forced to migrate from the theatre to the silver screen.[15]

Zapin in the Malay Movies

Like the other Malay folk dances that were already popular with the patron-dancers in the *joget* dance stages and cabarets, *zapin* was considered by the dance instructors and choreographers in the film companies as a versatile dance tradition that could be choreographed for the movies. The introduction of Western and Latin musical instruments in *zapin* performances on the *ronggeng* stages and in the cabarets allowed for more innovations in *zapin* as these musical instruments enabled the incorporation of foreign tunes into *zapin* music. Since scenes in the movies varied from the make-believe fantasy of heavenly beings to realistic depictions of real-life situations, choreographers had ample room for creativity. Some of the dances were produced specifically for certain scenes and were entirely made up of movements borrowed from Latin and Malay dance traditions. In most instances, choreographers who were already familiar with Malay folk dances would choreograph dances for the movies based upon Malay folk dances. The performance of *zapin* which often took place in the royal throne room, or the Balairongseri of the Malay Sultans, in the *bangsawan* theatre was re-enacted in the movies.

The technical capabilities of film-making, and, in particular, the use of multi-camera shots, enabled separate dance sequences to be choreographed for different cameras at different times. Thus, a dance piece was choreographed in several sections which were performed at different times by either the same or different groups of dancers according to the filming schedules.[16] The breaking of dance sequences into sections allowed choreographers more flexibility in making changes and innovations whenever these were required by the directors. Film-making also allowed a single dance to be shot several times. Although this was convenient for film editing and for the choreographers, it was hard on the dancers. When a single dance had to be performed several times on camera, the pressure to sustain a lively performance throughout the entire filming session often caused dancers fatigue. However, this could be avoided by scheduling the shootings at different times to allow the dancers time to recuperate.

The *zapin* dance sequence in a movie often served as a chorus dance sequence. The prima donna, who was either the movie heroine or the lead dancer, would perform separate dance motives at specific intervals during the chorus. This not only enabled the prima donna to disengage herself from the chorus line when she had to sing the song to which the dance was an accompaniment, but it also provided a multiple perspective of the dance performance.[17] Therefore, it was possible for the choreographers to teach different sets of *zapin* dance motives to the prima donna and the chorus line, and yet have them performed together during a single camera shot or at different camera angles.

As in the *bangsawan* theatre, *zapin* dances in the Malay movies were used to portray grand dance formations in the Sultan's court. However, an advantage of performing *zapin* on camera was the abandonment of the restrictive linear dance formations imposed by the limitations of the *bangsawan* stage. Dancers were able to perform the *zapin* in numerous dance formations without offending or embarrassing the audience because the movie cameras could avoid shots of the dancers' backs or unacceptable profiles. The cameramen, aided by the camera scripts, were responsible for obtaining proper footage of dances. This technical advance not only relieved the dancers of the burden of conforming to social decorum, but also for the first time allowed the dances to be viewed from several angles. *Zapin* dances were also filmed from above, a technique which revealed numerous floor formations which were not visible when the dance was viewed at ground level.[18] The availability of a bird's eye view encouraged *zapin* instructors and choreographers to innovate and create new dance motives and floor plans. *Zapin* choreography became more interesting when choreographers created new *zapin* dances with ideas borrowed from other dance traditions.

The Principals: The Mid-1950s to the 1960s

By the middle of the 1950s, more Malay movie directors and assistant directors were being appointed. Malay movie directors who were appointed by Shaw Brothers for MFP were P. Ramlee, Jamil Sulong, Omar Rojik, and S. Kadarisman. Cathay Kris appointed S. Roomai Noor, M. Amin, Hussein Haniff, Nordin Ahmad, Salleh Ghani, and Mat Sentol.[19] Almost all the Malay movie directors had, however, learned the art of movie-making from the Indian movie directors, either through some form of formal training or by apprenticeship. Some of the Malay movie directors themselves acted in their movies.

P. Ramlee, for example, became one of the best known movie actors in the history of the Malay movies. He was an exemplary director–actor who had acted in one hundred films that he himself had directed before his death from heart failure in 1973.[20] He had become a movie director after serving an apprenticeship to the Indian movie directors from whom he learned the technical aspects of movie-directing. P. Ramlee was also an excellent singer and songwriter. He was first employed by MFP in Singapore as a cover singer, his voice being used for the songs of actors such as Osman Gumanti, S. Roomai Noor, and M. Amin. His first role as a movie star was as the hero in a movie entitled *Takdir Illahi* (God's Will), directed by L. Krishnan.

P. Ramlee and other Malay movie directors were more sensitive than the Indian directors to the rightful representation of Malay culture in Malay movies. They realized that successful movies depended not only on the employment of star actors and actresses but also on good

A section of the Jalan Ampas movie studio. This was where P. Ramlee spent his career as a movie star and director with Shaw Brothers' Malay Film Production. It was also the venue where new dances from the *joget*, *inang*, *asli*, and *zapin* genres were choreographed.

P. Ramlee playing the violin while accompanying the actress Siput Sarawak in a dance in the movie *Racun Dunia* directed by B. S. Rajhan.

3 In the movie *Ibu*, P. Ramlee played the trumpet in a scene depicting a combo performing in a cab

4 P. Ramlee dressed as an Arab playing the mandolin in the movie *Ali Baba Bujang Lapuk* in 1960.
dress and the mandolin (perhaps representing the *'ud*) were supposed to create a Middle Eas
ambience.

5 P. Ramlee and Zaiton dancing in the movie *Anakku Sazali* directed by Phani Majumdar in 1956.

P. Ramlee and D. Harris performing a dance with their respective partners in the movie *Nasib* under the direction of B. S. Rajhan.

7 The *gambus*, with its short, fretless neck and wooden, pear-shaped body, is derived from the Middle Eastern *'ud*.

8 The harmonium (left), an organ-like keyboard instrument with small metal reeds and a pair of bellows operated by hand, is borrowed from Indian music tradition.

The *marwas* hand drum is a double-headed cylindrical drum with a very shallow body; the skins are attached to the body by laces of (nylon) rope.

The *dok* has a much longer body than the *marwas*.

11 A bronze, single-knob gong.

12 A *Zapin Melayu* music ensemble.

13 An evening *joget lambak* performance in an open space in Malacca in the 1970s.

14 *Joget lambak* musicians playing *joget* songs.

15   An all-female *zapin* dance group performing in a linear position. Arm swaying is restricted to the right arm while the left holds the

scripts, well-written and well-arranged songs, and superbly choreographed dances. All these artistic requirements had to be fulfilled in
order to attract a larger audience and thus compete with other movies.
While P. Ramlee wrote numerous songs for the movies, he also encouraged dancers to create new dance motives. There were only a few
good dancer–choreographers who were also good actors and actresses.
Osman Gumanti was one such actor. P. Ramlee encouraged some
actresses such as Normadiah, Saadiah, and Rahmah Rahmat to create
new dance styles and to innovate on the dances.

Normadiah became one of the most creative dance choreographers
in the Malay movie industry. Like most of the movie dancers, she was
familiar with the music and dances of the *bangsawan* theatre. Rahmah
Rahmat, a former movie actress and dancer, attributed Normadiah's
success to her ability to produce choreography of the highest standard
in each of her movies. Normadiah was known to be a strict dance
instructor who would go to great lengths to perfect her choreography.
She demanded the same kind of dedication from her dancers and
would often throw tantrums when she found them performing below
the standard that she expected.[21]

The drive towards better dance repertoires and professionalism
among dancers, instructors, choreographers, and directors contributed
to the rapid development of new choreography in all the dances performed in Malay movies. This was further enhanced by the borrowing
of dance motives from popular Latin dances. The choreographers
continued the tradition of creating new dance motives from foreign
sources as the former *bangsawan* choreographers such as Minah Yem,
Minah B, Ainon Chik, and Zaharah Agus had done. The movie
industry not only encouraged new dance repertoires but also provided
the opportunity for making these new dance styles popular with the
public.

Aziz Sattar, a former movie director–actor–comedian with Shaw
Brothers who was a close friend of P. Ramlee, commented that it was
people like P. Ramlee who made music-making and dance choreography a challenge in the Malay movies.[22] Whenever their songs and
dances became popular with the public, it became necessary to create
even better compositions.

The versatility of the choreographers who created the new *zapin*
dance motives that were portrayed in the movies encouraged dancers
and instructors in schools and social clubs all over the country to create
and add variations to their *zapin* performances. Several new motives
shown in movies eventually became standard motives in the new *zapin*
because they were repeated so often in the movies. Not only did the
new repertoires become standard, they also became synonymous with
the nation-wide version of the *zapin* dance. The Malay movie industry
had unintentionally given rise to the development of contemporary
zapin. The directors and choreographers, in perfecting the dances in
Malay movies, were indirectly responsible for the spread of the new
version of the genre to the public. By the early 1960s, the new *zapin*

had already become the national version performed by all groups of
performers in Malaysia.

The Demise of the Old *Zapin*

When the new *zapin* dance became the standard national version in the
late 1950s and the early 1960s, the village version, *Zapin Melayu*, was
precluded from national exposure. *Zapin Melayu* remains one of the
regional dance traditions which is only performed in the villages for
specific occasions by the local population of the area in which the
tradition survives. The *Zapin Melayu* of Johore that once shared performance characteristics similar to the *zapin* dance traditions of the
alam Melayu (Malay world) was eclipsed by the technological power
of the modern mass media. The *bangsawan* theatre, the *ronggeng* and
joget dance stages, and the urban entertainment parks have all been
instrumental, since the 1930s, in changing the course of *Zapin Melayu*
in Malaysia. The Malay movie industry, which was a popular public
entertainment medium from the 1950s to the mid-1960s, and later
television were the media by which the national version of the *zapin*
was disseminated to the public at large.

Perhaps the greatest irony of all is that *Zapin Melayu*, which was the
source for the creation of contemporary *zapin*, has never really spread
beyond the traditional Malay villages of north-west Johore. *Zapin Melayu*,
which belongs to the period of the older Malay world, is destined to
remain there. Although its performance styles and basic dance phrases
are similar to those of the *zapin* of Penyengat in the Riau Islands, Siak
Sri Indrapura, and Deli and Serdang in East Sumatra, *Zapin Melayu*
today remains a regional dance of north-west Johore. The names of
some of its dance motives, although similar to those in the Riau Islands
and East Sumatra, remain localized in north-west Johore and are
unknown to the rest of the *zapin* community in Malaysia.

Even its role as the traditional entertainment for social functions in
the Johore villages of Muar, Lenga, and Batu Pahat has been on the
decline. Efforts to revitalize the tradition of *Zapin Melayu* in north-west
Johore are minimal in comparison to the attention given to the contemporary *zapin* tradition throughout the country. Perhaps one of the
reasons for its decline is the redundancy of its dance motives. The less
challenging dance motives, the repetitive nature of the dance sequences,
and the simpler dance floor plans may explain why *Zapin Melayu* has
lost popularity to contemporary *zapin*.

As more complicated dance motives have been introduced in *zapin*
since its inception in Malay popular culture in the 1930s, *zapin* has
been accorded a recognition almost equal to that of other dances performed by the public at urban entertainment parks. The *zapin* that was
initially promoted for commercial exploitation has become a popular
dance tradition, whereas *Zapin Melayu*, which was initially the source
for dance choreography in the *bangsawan* theatre, and the basis for the
dance repertoire on the *ronggeng* or *joget* dance stages, has remained as

a village tradition. The new *zapin* which developed from the older tradition of *Zapin Melayu* was never named *Zapin Melayu* but became known as the *zapin* dance: only the word *zapin* remains as a reminder of its village origin. The new dance form that emerged has been transformed into a popular dance tradition which is performed not only in Malaysia and Singapore but also in southern Thailand.

1. During the pre-war period Malay newspapers such as *Warta Malaya, Saudara,* and *Warta Jenaka* with its movie column Ruangan Alam Cinema covered Malay movies. The coverage included news about new movies, movie stars, and even reviews of the movies shown (Wan Abdul Kadir, *Budaya Popular dalam Masyarakat Melayu Bandaran,* Kuala Lumpur: Dewan Bahasa dan Pustaka, Kementerian Pendidikan Malaysia, 1988, pp. 171–95). In the 1950s and 1960s, popular periodicals such as *Dunia Filem, Majalah Filem,* and *Movie News* became popular sources of the latest gossip about movie stars, local *haute couture,* and the most up-to-date news on films produced.

2. Abi, *Filem Melayu Dahulu dan Sekarang,* Shah Alam: Marwilis Publisher, 1987, p. 6.

3. These were the Happy World, the New World, and the Great World entertainment parks in Singapore.

4. Sharifah Zinjuaher H. M. Ariffin and Hang Tuah Arshad, *Sejarah Filem Melayu,* Kuala Lumpur: Penerbitan Sri Sharifah, 1980, p. 24.

5. Abi, op. cit., pp. 10–11.

6. Sharifah Zinjuaher and Hang Tuah, op. cit., pp. 24–5.

7. Erik Barnouw and S. Krishnaswamy, *Indian Film,* New York: Oxford University Press, 1980, p. 155.

8. Abi, op. cit., pp. 6–7.

9. Sharifah Zinjuaher and Hang Tuah, op. cit., pp. 24–5.

10. Personal interview with Dato L. Krishnan, August 1989.

11. P. Ramlee copied the story from an Indian movie and added the melodramatic nuances which were familiar to Malay movie viewers. He himself played the part of the protagonist, the trishaw peddler. (Personal interview with Dato L. Krishnan, August 1989.)

12. Abi, op. cit., p. 11.

13. P. Ramlee's name at birth was Teuku Zakaria bin Teuku Nyak Puteh. He was the son of an Acehnese migrant from Sumatra who had settled in Penang, Malaysia. His interest in music was enhanced during the Japanese occupation of Malaya when he learned to play the piano, the violin, and the ukelele from a Japanese music teacher. After the Second World War, P. Ramlee played in numerous stage and talent shows in Penang. In 1948, he was spotted by B. S. Rajhan, the Indian movie director from Singapore, at a talent show. His song entitled 'Azizah' (believed to be the name of his sweetheart) became his first hit in the same year. In the 1950s and the 1960s, P. Ramlee became the most popular Malay songwriter and composer in Malaysia. The P. Ramlee Memorial set up by the Malaysian government after his death houses memorabilia pertaining to his contributions to the world of Malay movies and music.

14. P. Ramlee used to suggest to the dance instructors the kind of new dance motives that could be created for the Malay dances in the movies. He was known to have a keen interest in the dances which he often saw in the cabarets that he and his friends frequented. It is believed that some of the *zapin* dance motives today were created by the movie studio's dance instructors at his suggestion.

15. Mustapha Kamil Yassin, 'The Malay Bangsawan', in Mohd Taib Osman (ed.), *Traditional Drama and Music of Southeast Asia,* Kuala Lumpur: Dewan Bahasa dan Pustaka, Kementerian Pelajaran Malaysia, 1974, p. 153.

16. Personal interview with Rahmah Rahmat in Singapore, August 1989.

17. This was the most common method of filming the song-and-dance sequences in the Malay movies produced in the 1950s and the early 1960s. The desire of the movie directors to create a collage of dance motives with the lead singer, who was usually the prima donna, appearing between the motives may perhaps have been due to the influence of the Hindustani movies.

18. This was one of the techniques employed by the camera crew to record the aerial view of dancers in circular and arabesque floor formations (personal interview with Dato L. Krishnan, August 1989).

19. Abi, op. cit., p. 12.

20. Because P. Ramlee was an excellent singer, musician, songwriter, actor, and director, he became the most versatile film star in the 1950s and the early 1960s. As a movie director, he was known to be a perfectionist who studied the elements of cinematography that would be most beneficial for his movies. The title Seniman Agung (The Great Artist) was bestowed on him by the people of Malaysia for his contribution to the field of Malay entertainment arts.

21. Personal interview with Rahmah Rahmat in Singapore, August 1989.

22. Personal interview with Aziz Sattar, August 1989.

6
Village and Contemporary *Zapin*:
The Music and Dance

The Performance Style

IN Johore and other parts of Peninsular Malaysia, *zapin* music, whether in its folk or contemporary version, is performed by small ensembles of six or seven men. In its staged version, the musicians are usually seated in a row behind and to one side of the dance area, depending on the availability of space. However, in a village setting, the musicians often sit on the floor in a semi-circle or small cluster in a space immediately adjacent to the dance area. During the *gambus* solo introductory passage the dancers often wait, crouching or kneeling on one knee, in front of and facing the *gambus* player. A virtuoso *gambus* player normally utilizes this unmetred *taksim*[1] section to display his skills at improvisation. The length of the solo *gambus* introductory *taksim* varies according to the personal preference of the *gambus* player. Sometimes he may lengthen the *taksim* in order to demonstrate his skills to an appreciative audience.

After the completion of the *taksim*, *Zapin Melayu* dancers begin the salutation dance phrase, which is similar to the *salam pembukaan* dance phrase of Penyengat and East and North Sumatra. Although the salutation dance is mandatory in *Zapin Melayu*, it is optional in the contemporary performance and is sometimes omitted.

In *Zapin Melayu*, the second section of the dance follows the salutation dance sequence. In contemporary *zapin*, the dance proper may begin immediately after the dancers appear on the stage; that is, when the salutation dance is not performed. The sequence of dances in the main section of the dance proper is the same in *Zapin Melayu* and contemporary *zapin*. The various dance sequences of the *ragam* (design or pattern), the *pecah* (breaks or fragmentations), and the *langkah* (steps or strides) are linked or connected to one another by the *gerak asas* (basic movements). When all the dance sequences selected for a *zapin* performance have been completed, the dancers may repeat successive cycles of similar dance sequences as long as the musicians keep playing the music.

The final section of the *zapin* dance is marked by the *wainab* segment, which is similar to the *tahtim* or *tahto* dance sequence found in Sumatra, the Riau Islands, and Singapore. The *wainab* serves as the coda for the dance and is marked by the loud interlocking rhythmic pattern known as the *kopak* of the *marwas* hand drums. The dancers perform movements which consist of variations of skips, turns, low *plié*, and standing and squatting positions. At the end of the four measures of the interlocking rhythmic pattern of the *marwas*, the dancers kneel swiftly with one knee on the ground and the other knee bent with the foot firmly on the ground. The same movement sequence may be repeated several times.

In its village or traditional setting, the melody of a *zapin* piece is carried by a vocalist, as well as the *gambus*, the violin, the harmonium, or the accordion. Following usual performance practice, any combination of these instruments may be used to carry the melody. The accordion and the violin are essentially the Western forms of these instruments. The *gambus*, however, is derived from the Middle Eastern *'ud*. Its short, fretless neck and wooden, pear-shaped body, which is rounded at the back, carry five to eight strings in double courses and a single high string. This lute is held horizontally in the player's lap and the strings are plucked with the fingers. The harmonium, an organ-like keyboard instrument with small metal reeds and a pair of bellows operated by hand, is borrowed from the Indian music tradition.

In a village orchestra, the drum part is played on the *marwas* hand drums, often punctuated by an additional drum called the *dok*. The *marwas* is a double-headed, cylindrical drum with a very shallow body. The skins are attached to the body by laces of rope (nylon rope being frequently used today) which are tied tightly to make the skin taut. In performance, only one head is struck with the fingers of one hand while the drum is held in the other hand. In *Zapin Melayu*, the three or four *marwas* drums play an interlocking style of drumming in which each player contributes specific drum sounds at specific times and in a specific rhythm to produce one complete or composite rhythmic pattern.

The second kind of drum in *Zapin Melayu*, called the *dok*, is also a cylindrical drum but with a much longer body than the *marwas* and with only one head which is struck by the fingers of one hand. The *dok* plays only certain beats of a given *marwas* rhythmic pattern, often punctuating specific upbeats or off-beats. The *dok* provides greater dynamism to the already syncopated rhythmic patterns set up by the *marwas* section.

In contrast to the musical instruments and the method of playing these instruments in *Zapin Melayu*, contemporary *zapin* orchestras found in large urban areas have become both more Westernized and more Malay in nature. A well-known ensemble in Kuala Lumpur, directed by the performer Ahmad Fadzil,[2] illustrates this apparent contradiction. In a 1985 recording of the *zapin* piece entitled 'Lancang Kuning', Fadzil has retained the violin, accordion, and *gambus*, but has also added the flute, thereby enlarging the melody-carrying section of the orchestra. On the percussion side, Fadzil has used only the deep-pitched *dok* drum from the village orchestra, while adding a *rebana* drum, a tambourine, and a single gong. The *rebana* is a single-headed, frame drum, the skin of which is attached to the body by rattan laces and made taut by wooden pegs inserted between the body and a cane ring located at the bottom end of the body. The drum is held upright in the player's lap and struck with the hands. The gong used in Fadzil's orchestra is a bronze, single-knobbed gong which is hung vertically and struck on the knob with a padded beater. The pitch of the gong is not necessarily related to the tuning of the other instruments in the ensemble nor to the tonal centre of a given piece. Its function is primarily that of a time marker in the music.

There are also differences between *Zapin Melayu* and contemporary *zapin* in the manner of performing dance sequences. The older *Zapin Melayu* subscribes to a more controlled way of dancing, the upper torso being kept almost rigidly upright with one arm behind the back or in front of the navel, and the other arm free to move. Contemporary *zapin* is more relaxed in that the torso is less rigid, while both arms are allowed freedom of movement corresponding to the movements of the feet. The most remarkable difference between the two forms of *zapin* is in the basic dance phrase. The basic dance phrase or *gerak asas* of *Zapin Melayu* is marked by the absence of leg movements at the first count of the dance phrase. In every measure of the basic dance phrase, the dancer remains in a stationary position at the first count (or beat) and then resumes movements on the second, third, and fourth counts. There is a marked departure from this style of dance movements in contemporary *zapin*. All the basic dance movements in contemporary *zapin* involve leg movements and the corresponding swaying of the arms. The first, second, and third counts of the basic dance phrase are filled with alternate leg movements in a stepping motion. At the fourth count of the basic dance phrase, the leg movements are marked by a 'side low' leg gesture.[3] This pattern is repeated in two to four measures before a variation of the dance sequence commences. The differences in the dance styles of *Zapin Melayu* and contemporary *zapin* and the differences in their respective styles of musical expression make *zapin* a dance of two traditions, one antiquated and one modern.

Zapin Music: The Structure

The following *Zapin Melayu* songs are frequently played in Lenga, Muar, and Batu Pahat:

Malay title:	English translation:
'Lagu Zapin Maulana'	*Zapin* Song of Maulana[4]
	(The Respected One)
'Lagu Gambus Jodoh'	*Gambus* Song of Love
'Lagu Gambus Kelantan'	Song of the *'Ud* of Kelantan
'Lagu Sikah Masri'	Song of *Sikah*[5] *Masri*
'Lagu Ya Salam'	Song of Greetings
'Lagu Anak Ayam'	Song of the Chicks
'Lagu Lancang Kuning'	Song of the Yellow Yacht
'Lagu Sikah'	Song of *Sikah*
'Lagu Sejahtera Watan'	Song of Harmonious Country

Another *zapin* song entitled 'Lagu Gambus Pontianak' (Song of the *'Ud* from Pontianak in Kalimantan) can no longer be played today because none of the musicians interviewed could remember the melody. A number of the older men who used to listen to *gambus* music or watch the *zapin* being performed when they were young boys remembered that it was frequently played in *zapin* performances during the early decades of the twentieth century. Of all the songs listed above, 'Lagu Zapin Maulana' is most frequently played in Lenga (see Appendix A.1). 'Lagu Gambus Palembang' is more popular in Muar (see Appendix A.2), while 'Lagu Sikah Masri' is often played in Batu Pahat (see Appendix A.3).

All the songs which today accompany the contemporary *zapin* dance are available on commercially produced audio cassette tapes:

Malay title:[6]	English translation:	Recording company:[7]
'Lancang Kuning'	Yellow Yacht	WEA and CBS
'Naamsidi' (Ar.)	Yes, Sir	Warner Bros and CBS
'Kamarulzaman' (Ar.)	Moon of the Century	Warner Bros
'Yaladan'	(meaning unknown)	Warner Bros
'Pantun Budi'	Quatrain of Kindness	WEA
'Gambus Palembang'	*'ud* of Palembang	WEA
'Salatollah' (Ar.)	Greetings to Allah	CBS
'Sireh Pinang'	Betel Leaves and Areca Nuts	Warner Bros and CBS

To illustrate the differences in the two traditions, the performances by groups in two different localities of a *zapin* song well known throughout the Malay world, and frequently played in *zapin* performances, are compared. Aspects of the two versions of this song, 'Lancang Kuning' (Yellow Yacht) make clear the characteristics which distinguish *Zapin Melayu* from contemporary *zapin*. Representative of the old tradition of *Zapin Melayu* is a rendition of the piece performed by a village *zapin* group from Batu Pahat (see Appendix A.4), while the version representative of *zapin* as a national folk idiom was performed by the *zapin* group led by Ahmad Fadzil (see Appendix A.5).

The Drum Rhythmic Pattern

Certain similarities and differences in the basic structural features of the drum rhythmic patterns and melodies of 'Lancang Kuning' are evident in the two *zapin* versions. Consider first the drum rhythmic patterns: in the village version, there are two different drumming patterns. The first pattern is four beats long and repeats with some slight variations throughout the piece (Figure 6.1). This pattern is played at the centre and edge of the drum head, using the individual fingers of one hand to achieve timbres in the medium and low ranges which are possible on the *marwas* drum.

FIGURE 6.1

Zapin Melayu: 'Lancang Kuning' (Batu Pahat) Four-beat Drum Pattern

(i) Basic patterns showing the three drum parts

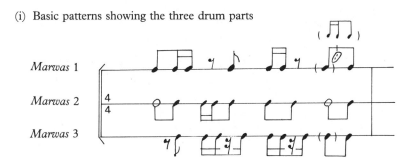

(ii) Basic composite pattern (as heard in performance)

Key:

♩ = medium range pitch, played at the edge of the drum head

♩ = low pitch, played near the middle of the drum head

As Figure 6.1 shows, this first four-beat pattern is played by three *marwas* drums in an interlocking style. The first and third *marwas* provide some rhythmic variation on the basic pattern (the variable drum strokes being shown in parentheses). The second *marwas* player, however, rarely deviates from his basic pattern and in addition he provides the low pitch heard consistently on the first half of beats one and four. The pattern is end-accented by agogic accent (that is, the length of the final note) or by a low pitch on the final note. The basic pattern or a variation of it is repeated throughout most of the piece.

The second drumming pattern, called the *kopak*, is made up of a total of twelve beats (or three bars in 4/4 time) (Figure 6.2) and is played loudly. The upper part of the palm of the hand is used to strike the centre of the drum head to achieve a very loud, sharp, clap-like timbre.

FIGURE 6.2

Zapin Melayu: 'Lancang Kuning' (Batu Pahat) Twelve-beat Drum Pattern

(i) Basic pattern showing the three drum parts

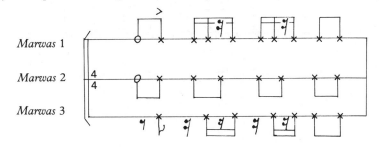

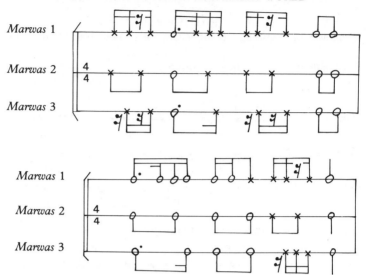

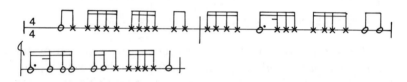

(ii) Composite pattern (as heard in performance)

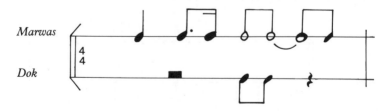

This second, contrasting, three-bar loud drumming pattern occurs only at specific points in the piece, notably at the end of a sung verse. Both patterns (the four-beat and the twelve-beat) are introduced immediately after the *gambus* improvisatory solo—the *taksim*—and before the sung verses begin.

In contrast to the traditional version from Batu Pahat, Fadzil's group plays only one drum rhythmic pattern (Figure 6.3), repeating it throughout the piece. Fadzil's four-beat drum pattern is played on only one *rebana* and one *dok*. This pattern is introduced at the very beginning of the piece and no solo *gambus* introduction is played.

FIGURE 6.3
Contemporary *Zapin*: 'Lancang Kuning' (Kuala Lumpur)
Four-beat Drum Pattern

Marwas

Dok

This pattern, utilizing far less sixteenth-note motion than the village group, is repeated throughout the piece and is not played in an interlocking style of drumming. Fadzil's four-beat drum pattern is marked on every main beat by the tambourine and it sounds as if it is marked at the end by the gong. However, the gong marker in relation to the melody actually falls on the first beat of a four-beat unit. Thus, one hears that Fadzil has shifted the traditional marking function of the gong from the end of a given rhythmic unit, found in much of traditional Malay music, to the beginning of the unit in his contemporary rendition of the piece.

In the village version, 'Lancang Kuning' opens with the *taksim*, a *gambus* improvised solo. This is followed immediately by the introduction of the traditional *zapin* rhythmic and melodic pattern and then it proceeds directly into the sung main section of the piece. In the national form, there is no introductory solo. In fact, there is no *gambus* and no vocal part. The melody in the main section of the piece in the national form is purely instrumental.

The Melody

In both versions of this piece the melody of the main section is cast in a three-part form: A, B, and C. The melodic sections A, B, and C, in both versions, consist of a specific number of smaller melodic phrases. This can be illustrated as follows (the bar numbers refer to the music transcriptions in Appendices A.4 and A.5).

In the village version: section A has two four-bar phrases (bars 8–11 and 13–16); section B has two three-bar phrases (bars 18–20 and 22–4); and section C has two two-bar phrases (bars 25–6 and 27–8).

In the national version: section A has two four-bar phrases (bars 5–8 and 9–12); section B has two five-bar phrases (bars 13–17 and 18–22); and section C has two four-bar phrases (bars 23–6 and 27–30).

In both versions, the three melodic sections, A, B, and C, are distinguished from each other by their tonal centre. For example, in the village version a given tonal centre is established in section A (notated as C in Appendix A.4) and section B uses the same tonal centre but with a lowered seventh scale degree (B). In contrast, section C establishes a new tonal centre at a perfect fourth (F) above that of sections A and B.

In the national version, the first two sections, A and B, use two different tonal centres a perfect fifth apart (G to D as notated in the music transcription in Appendix A.5). Section C uses the same tonal centre as section B but with the lowered third and seventh scale degrees. It is interesting to note that in the national version, only section B approximates the traditional melody of the piece 'Lancang Kuning'. This perhaps points to a great deal of melodic improvisation in the national form; the original 'Lancang Kuning' melody is almost unrecognizable. Nevertheless, Fadzil still maintains a basic three-part form in the overall melodic pattern along with the use of the lowered seventh scale degree in the tonal vocabulary. The tonal relationships among the major melodic sections, however, use the perfect fifth relationship (instead of the perfect fourth as in the village form). Within these parameters, he improvises, using both old and new melodies in the piece.

Another significant difference between the two versions is that in the village form the singer, *gambus,* and violin are used in every strophe or verse throughout the piece. The instrumentation and the use of the voice are constant. In the national form, however, the flute, violin, and accordion are featured as the principal melody carriers, each instrument taking up each section, A, B, and C, alternately from one strophe or verse to another. The combination of instruments playing is constantly changing.

Summary

The performance of village *zapin* always begins with an improvised *gambus* solo—the *taksim*—and this is followed immediately by the introduction of the traditional *gambus* melody and rhythm played by the *gambus* and drum ensemble (Figure 6.4). Thereafter, the singer carries the melody and song through a complete verse, the ABC unit (A, B, and C sections), and this, in turn, is immediately followed by the three-bar loud *kopak* pattern of the *marwas* drums. These two sections—the ABC unit and the three-bar loud *kopak* pattern—alternate to the end of the piece. The piece concludes with an extended form of the three-bar loud *kopak* pattern and a final cadence in the *wainab* or *tahtim* section.

FIGURE 6.4

Zapin Melayu Music: Summary

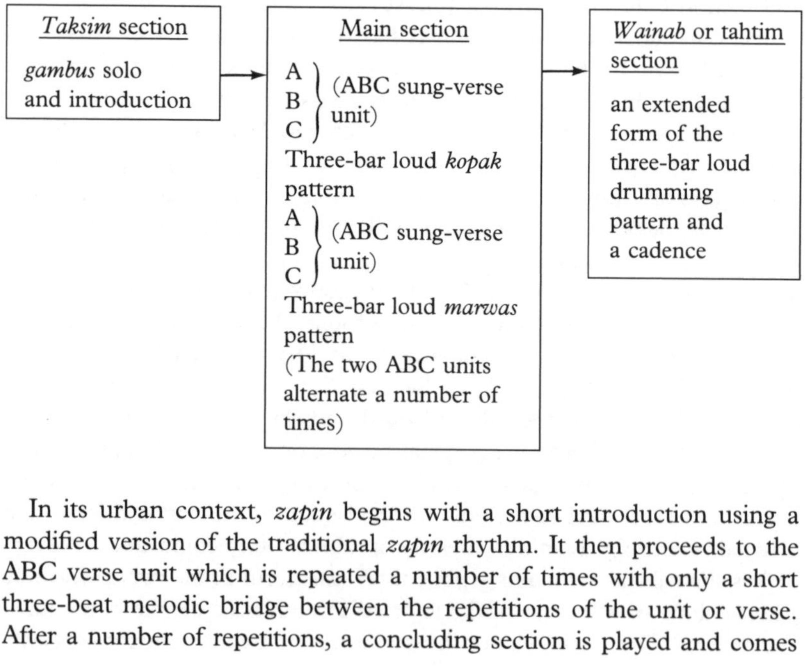

Taksim section	Main section	*Wainab* or tahtim section
gambus solo and introduction	A, B, C (ABC sung-verse unit) — Three-bar loud *kopak* pattern — A, B, C (ABC sung-verse unit) — Three-bar loud *marwas* pattern (The two ABC units alternate a number of times)	an extended form of the three-bar loud drumming pattern and a cadence

In its urban context, *zapin* begins with a short introduction using a modified version of the traditional *zapin* rhythm. It then proceeds to the ABC verse unit which is repeated a number of times with only a short three-beat melodic bridge between the repetitions of the unit or verse. After a number of repetitions, a concluding section is played and comes to an abrupt end. Then, as if to make sure the listener really knows that the piece is a *zapin* piece, the accordion and the percussion section play a four-bar rendition of the old, traditional *zapin* melody and the drum rhythmic pattern. Figure 6.5 summarizes the format of contemporary *zapin* music.

FIGURE 6.5

Contemporary *Zapin* Music: Summary

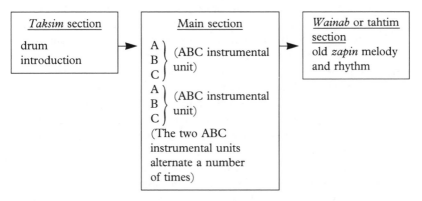

Zapin Dance: The Structure

The differences and subtle similarities of the two *zapin* traditions are not only reflected in the musical form of the genre but extended into the dance performance. The *Zapin Melayu* dance is different in style of performance from contemporary *zapin*. The performance style of both the old and the new *zapin* traditions is governed by the manner of dancing the *gerak asas* or basic dance phrase and the formation of all the dance variations in a network of sequences and dance motives.

A dance phrase is formed by a synthesis of dance movements. A number of dance motives may form a dance sequence. The completed dance motives are connected to each other by the *gerak asas* or basic dance phrase. Dance motives are like the foliation of a dance pattern in space and time.

All the dance phrases of the two dance traditions are contained within the structure of the *gerak asas* peculiar to the particular *zapin* tradition. However, it must be noted that the two traditions discussed here are similar to the *zapin* dances found all over the Malay world in that the dance is formulated in three sections. The first dance section is the salutional dance phrase. The second section forms the main dance segment in the repertoire and corresponds to the main section of the *zapin* music. The third and final section of the dance is the *wainab* section which corresponds to the *tahtim* or *tahto* section of the *zapin* dance of Singapore, the Riau Islands, and Siak and Serdang in Sumatra.

The *Zapin Melayu* dance begins with the *taksim*[8] musical prelude— an improvised solo by *gambus*, violin, or harmonium. The free unmetred section of the *taksim* serves as an introduction to the dance proper. During the *taksim*, dancers wait either outside the dance area or in position in the dance area, assuming the half-kneeling, half-squatting salutation posture of the *sembah* (homage) or *salam* (greetings). There are variations to the salutation posture from one *Zapin Melayu* group to another. In contemporary *zapin*, when the *taksim* section is replaced with an introductory drum sequence, the period of the salutation posture may be shorter than that of *Zapin Melayu*. In some cases, the salutational dance phrase may be performed during the first few dance phrases in the main section of the *zapin* song, totally severing the *taksim* section from the dance performance.

The melodic section following the *taksim* serves as the main dance section of the *zapin* repertoire. It consists of several clusters of dance motives repeated several times until the main section of the *zapin* music rises into a coda in the concluding section of the *wainab*. The dance motives are clustered within the ABC units of the 'Lancang Kuning' piece. The ABC unit, repeated a number of times, serves as the cyclic core for the alternate repetitions of dance motives. A *zapin* dance motive is made up of several dance phrases.

The *wainab*[9] section of the dance is the coda, which corresponds to the *tahtim* or *tahto* section of the music. This dance section forms a finale which is marked by a variation of skips, turns, low *plié*, and standing and squatting positions performed at a faster speed than the rest of the dance routine. The *wainab* section is terminated when the dancers return to the *sembah* (homage) or *salam* (greetings) salutation position at the end of the concluding phrase of the *zapin* music. Figure 6.6 summarizes the format of the *zapin* dance.

FIGURE 6.6
The *Zapin* Dance: Summary

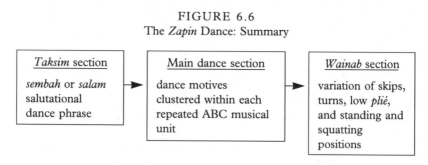

Taksim section	Main dance section	*Wainab* section
sembah or *salam* salutational dance phrase	dance motives clustered within each repeated ABC musical unit	variation of skips, turns, low *plié*, and standing and squatting positions

The Basic Dance Phrase (*Gerak Asas*)

Zapin Melayu

The *gerak asas* of village *zapin* or *Zapin Melayu* and contemporary *zapin* differs. The *gerak asas* is a rudimentary four-beat dance phrase involving stepping motions accompanied by the corresponding arm movements, and it is upon this that dance motives are created. The *gerak asas* of *Zapin Melayu* has a pause on the first dance count where all body movements are suspended. The dancer or dancers remain in the initial standing position.

It is only on the second dance count that actual stepping motions begin.

An example of the leg movements during a four-beat dance phrase is enumerated as follows:

on count 1, all movements are suspended;
on count 2, the left foot steps 'right-forward diagonal middle';
on count 3, the right foot steps 'left-forward diagonal middle'; and
on count 4, the left foot steps 'forward middle' (see Appendix B.1).

In the second section of the *gerak asas*, all four counts of the dance phrase are executed while the dancer makes a 180-degree turn to face the opposite direction:

on count 1, while the position of the left leg is held, the right foot swings behind the left foot as the torso turns 180 degrees;
on count 2, the right foot steps 'forward middle', while the left foot turns 180 degrees to the right;
on count 3, the left foot steps 'backward high', raising the body and the right foot; and
on count 4, both feet return to the floor, the left foot 'place middle', the right foot 'forward middle' (see Appendix B.1).

As mentioned earlier, the arm movements of *Zapin Melayu* are restricted to one arm only. The other hand is held at the back or in front of the waistline (see dance notation in Appendix B.1). The mobile hand sways forward and back with the elbow bent, putting the forearm in a 'forward middle' position. The fist is clenched with all four fingers curled into the palm. The thumb is pointed 'forward middle'. The arm movements are referred to as *satu terikat satu melenggang* which literally means 'one locked, the other sways'.

Contemporary Zapin

In contrast, the most striking feature of the *gerak asas* in contemporary *zapin* is the use of all four counts in a dance phrase. There are no pauses or holding back of bodily motions in any of the four counts. The *gerak asas* in contemporary *zapin* allows a continuous flow of body movements without the feeling of a sudden suspension of motion as in *Zapin Melayu*. The *gerak asas* in contemporary *zapin* can be enumerated as follows:

on count 1, the right foot steps 'forward middle';
on count 2, the left foot steps 'forward middle';
on count 3, the right foot steps 'forward middle'; and
on count 4, the left foot steps 'left side low', while the right leg supports the body (see Appendix B.2).

The *gerak asas* is repeated in lateral symmetry in the second dance phrase. There is, however, another variant of the *gerak asas* which involves a variation on the third and fourth counts of the dance phrase. Instead of the right foot stepping 'forward middle', it is placed next to the left foot, with the ball of the right foot supporting the body weight. Meanwhile, the left leg is bent forward with the foot firmly on the ground. Both feet provide body support. On the fourth count, the right leg remains in place with the left foot firmly on the ground supporting the body weight. With the body support on the right leg, the left leg moves to 'left side low' with the foot touching the ground. This can be enumerated as follows:

on count 1, the right foot steps 'forward middle';
on count 2, the left foot steps 'forward middle';
on count 3, the right foot steps in 'place low', the left foot in 'place low'; and
on count 4, the right foot holds in 'place middle', with support on the right leg, the left leg moves to 'left side low' (see Appendix B.3).

This variant of the *gerak asas* is also repeated in lateral symmetry in the second dance phrase. The *gerak asas* is performed within the four-beat phrase and can be repeated as many times as required. However, the norm is to repeat the *gerak asas* at least two times in order to allow each foot the chance of stepping out on the side. The regular, repeated, symmetrical pattern of a dance phrase forms the *gerak asas* dance sequence.

The arm movements also display a strong departure from the village tradition of *Zapin Melayu*. Instead of one arm being held close to the body and only the other arm being allowed to move, both arms in contemporary *zapin* move alternately in an opposing sequence, almost like a walking motion. The palms are in a closed position with the fingers curled into them. The arms sway horizontally to the body. The upper arm moves sideways to 'backward diagonal low' and proceeds to 'forward low', while the lower arm sways horizontally in front of the body to 'backward diagonal low' and returns to 'forward diagonal middle'. The arm movements correspond to the leg movements. When the right foot steps forward, the right arm sways to the back, while the left arm sways forward. This movement is repeated symmetrically by the left arm moving back as the right arm moves forward when the left foot steps forward. On count four, however, the arm that corresponds to the side-stepping leg moves to 'side low', while turning the wrist to face 'back low'. (See Appendix B.2.)

The Dance Motives

The dance motives of the two *zapin* versions are also different. The dance motives in both versions are known as *ragam tari* (dance pattern) or *bunga tari* (dance flowers). However, the *ragam tari* in *Zapin Melayu* is almost exclusively restricted to variations of the leg movements, while the arms retain the prescribed motion of 'one locked, the other sways' as in *satu terikat satu melenggang*. It is upon the *gerak asas* that the *ragam tari* in *Zapin Melayu* is constructed. The *ragam tari* in contemporary *zapin* is also based on the *gerak asas*, but differs from *Zapin Melayu* in that the fact that there is no suspension of bodily movements on the first dance count imbues a sense of continuous flow in each of the dance motives.

Variations of Dance Phrases in Zapin Melayu

The terminology used to identify some dance phrases of the *zapin* of Penyengat, Siak, and Serdang, other than the term *gerak asas*, is very similar to that of *Zapin Melayu*. All the terms for the *zapin* phrases are named after the stylized gestures that imitate actions of men or nature. The *zapin* groups in Lenga, Muar, and Batu Pahat in north-west Johore have an array of dance motives consisting of sequences of dance phrases identified under the variations of *sembah* (homage), *ragam* (pattern), *anak* (child), *lompat* (leap or jump), *pusau* (twirl), *pecah* (breaks or fragmentations), and *wainab* (meaning unknown but similar to the *tahtim/tahto* dance coda). A complete list of the variations of dance motives is as follows:

Malay title:	English translation:
Sembah (homage) variations:	
sembah duduk	homage in sitting position
berdiri langkah sebelah	standing with side step
langkah belakang	step to the back
Ragam (pattern) variations:	
ragam satu	pattern one
ragam dua	pattern two
ragam tiga	pattern three
ragam empat	pattern four
ragam lima	pattern five
ragam enam	pattern six
ragam langkah belakang	step to the back pattern
ragam siku keluang	flying fox's elbow pattern
Anak (child) variations:	
anak ayam	chicks, as in young chickens
anak ikan	fish fry (the young of fishes)
buang anak	throw a child
Lompat (leap or jump) variations:	
lompat kecil	small leaps
lompat Tiong	leaps of the hill myna bird
Pusau (twirl) variations:	
pusau belanak	twirls of the grey mullet fish
pusau belanak kecil	small twirls of the grey mullet fish
pusau belanak besar	larger twirls of the grey mullet fish
Pecah (breaks or fragmentations) variations:	
pecah dua	double fragmentations
pecah empat	four fragmentations
pecah enam	six fragmentations
pecah lapan	eight fragmentations
pecah sepuluh	ten breaks or fragmentations
pecah duabelas	twelve breaks or fragmentations

Wainab variations:

    tahto   (meaning unknown)

    tahtim   (meaning unknown)

It is important to note that some movements which have different names are similar. Good examples are the a*nak ikan* (fish fry) and the *buang anak* (throwing a child) dance motives. The former is also known as *songsang arus* (go against the current or flow) and the latter as *buang setapak* (throw a step). Another dance motive which does not belong to any of the movement varieties is the *sisip* (inserts or side shifts) dance sequence.

SEMBAH

All *sembah* (homage) dance motives in *Zapin Melayu* use the *salam* or greeting gestures which are similar to the *salam pembukaan* dance phrase in the *zapin* of Penyengat, Siak, and Serdang. The *sembah* dance motive is performed either in the half-kneeling, half-squatting position or in the standing position. The dancers' hands are held together with the palms touching each other and are raised in front towards the forehead, the nose, or the chest. (See Appendices B.4–B.5.)

RAGAM

Ragam dance motives in *Zapin Melayu* are more commonly performed in the Lenga area than in any other areas in north-west Johore. A basic *ragam* dance phrase begins with three counts of 'forward middle' steps beginning with the right leg. The dancers either hold movements on the fourth count or turn 180 degrees to face in the opposite direction. The differences between one *ragam* dance phrase and another are regulated by degrees of variation in the way turns are made in retracing the initial path of the dance floor plan. The *ragam* dance motive ranges from a two-measure to an eight-measure dance phrase. (See Appendices B.7–B.10.)

ANAK

The *anak* variety of dance motives in *Zapin Melayu* begins with the basic dance phrase, the *gerak asas*, in the first measure. Following this, the dancer takes diagonal and side steps while turning around in the second measure. The dancer then repeats the two measures to bring him back to where he started. In the *anak ayam* dance motive the dancer takes forward and backward steps while turning around in the second measure; on the first count of the second measure, the dancer's right foot touches the left heel before stepping into 'right-forward diagonal middle'. In the *anak ikan* dance motive, the right foot does not touch the left heel. (See Appendices B.11–B.12.)

LOMPAT

Lompat dance motives consist of hops, skips, or jumps which are usually performed during the *wainab* dance section of *Zapin Melayu*. The staccato movements of the legs, each taking turns to support the body while the other makes a kicking or thrusting-like gesture, are timed to coincide with the *kopak* drumming patterns of the *wainab* section of the *zapin* dance. (See Appendix B.13.)

PUSAU

The *pusau* dance motives trace the twirling motion of legs drawn on the floor. It is the relative size of the twirling motions that identifies each of the *pusau* variations. The standard *pusau* variation is the *pusau belanak*. The first measure of the dance motive consists of diagonal steps and turns which draw a twirl-like motion on the floor. This is followed in the second measure by steps and turns back to the starting place and dance position. The dance phrase is repeated at least once before other dance motives are commenced. The dance performers liken this movement to that of a fish stranded on a mud bank twirling towards the nearest water hole. The larger or smaller twirls of the variations are referred to as *pusau belanak besar* and *pusau belanak kecil* respectively. (See Appendix B.14.)

PECAH

The *pecah* dance motives in *Zapin Melayu* refer to the variation in the floor plans that results from the number of dancers performing the dance. Since all the dancers follow one pattern of dance variation at any given time, they display opposite movements when they dance facing one another. This is to say, when the dancers perform the same dance motives opposite one another, their movements towards and away from one another create a display of the merging and fragmentation of dance patterns. The *pecah* dance motives relate to the number of dancers performing one or several dance motives while facing each other either in two straight rows or in a circle. A *pecah* dance motive does not imply movements peculiar to a particular style or form but represents the breaking away of a merging group of dancers. When there are only two pairs of dancers performing the merging and breaking away formation, the *pecah* dance motive is known as *pecah dua* or double fragmentation. (See Appendix B.15.) Thus, the *pecah* dance motives are numbered in ascending order corresponding to the number of paired dancers performing the merging and breaking away dance floor plan. For example, four pairs of dancers would represent the *pecah empat* dance or four fragmentations dance motives.

SISIP

The *sisip* (inserts/side shifts) dance motive, as an exception, does not belong to any of the cluster of movement variations. The *sisip* dance motive consists of several measures of a combination of a 'forward diagonal' step and 'place middle' dance phrases. The dancer steps into a 'right-forward diagonal middle' with the left foot on the second count of the first dance phrase. He follows this by stepping into 'place middle' on the right foot and the left foot on the third and fourth counts of the dance phrase, with the torso facing 'right-forward diagonal'. The second dance phrase is a repeat of the first dance phrase but begins with the right foot stepping into 'left-forward diagonal middle'. The torso faces the 'left-forward diagonal'. By performing several measures of the *sisip* dance phrase, he constructs a sequence of movements with the torso facing 'forward diagonal' in alternate directions. The motion of facing 'forward diagonal' while moving in a straight line is likened to the insertion of sideway shifts while tracing a straight path. Hence the dance motive is referred to as the *sisip*. (See Appendix B.16.)

WAINAB

Wainab from different localities vary according to the local style of skips, hops, and fast crouching positions. Some variations of the *lompat tiong* dance phrase may be performed during the *wainab*. The *wainab* dance motives in *Zapin Melayu* may also consist of a variation of skips, hops, and fast crouching positions. Different groups from different localities may prefer more or fewer skips or hops in their *wainab* motives. It is important, however, to ensure a change in the flow of the *zapin* dance when the drummers perform the *kopak*, loud drum patterns, in the *wainab* section. It is at this point that the dancers dance with more vigour and more energy, a marked departure from the regulated flow of the dance sequences in the main body of the dance.

Variations of Dance Motives in Contemporary Zapin

The *ragam tari* (dance pattern) or *bunga tari* (dance flowers) in contemporary *zapin* are also based on the *gerak asas*, but unlike *Zapin Melayu*, they utilize all four dance counts for body movements in a single dance phrase. There is always a sense of continuous flow in each dance motive where the dance phrases are connected to one another with a forward- or side-stepping motion. In contrast to village *zapin*, the dance phrases that constitute one or several dance motives are not identified under a cluster of similarly titled dance phrase variations. Instead, the dance motives in contemporary *zapin* are identified under specific titles that denote specific dance formations. The dance motives that are commonly performed today are the following:

Malay title:	English translation:
langkah hadapan	forward steps
langkah belakang	backward steps
pusing kiri	left turn
pusing kanan	right turn
brek	brakes
siku keluang	flying fox's elbow
unta	camel
enjut	move up and down
zig-zak	zigzag
halang	obstruct

tepuk silat	*silat*[10] (martial art) claps
wainab	(meaning unknown)

LANGKAH AND *PUSING*

The *langkah hadapan* (forward steps), *langkah belakang* (backward steps), *pusing kiri* (left turn), and *pusing kanan* (right turn) dance motives of contemporary *zapin* consist of several measures of the *gerak asas* dance phrase performed in straight or circular dance paths. All the dancers of the contemporary tradition dance in pairs facing one another. Their forward steps lead them to face one another at a very close range at the end of the *langkah hadapan* dance motive. In the *langkah belakang* dance motive, the dancers retrace the initial dance path with backward steps, leading them further away from one another. The function of the *langkah hadapan* and *langkah belakang* dance motives is to merge the dancers, putting them flirtatiously close to one another, and then breaking them away from one another. (See Appendix B.17.) The *pusing kiri* and *pusing kanan* dance motives are usually performed when the dance partners facing one another make a right or left small circular path using the forward steps of the *gerak asas*. Each dancer dances around the circumference of his or her own circle. (See Appendix B.18.)

BREK

The *brek* (brakes/braking steps) dance motive involves brake-like steps after the first count of the first dance phrase. Instead of stepping into 'forward middle' on the left foot on the second count, the dancer steps into 'forward low' with the knees bent forward. He follows this by making a backward step on the right foot on the third count and lifting the left leg on the fourth count. The leg movements on the second and third counts of the dance phrase arrest or retard the forward motion of the body. Hence the term 'brek', derived from the English word 'brake'. In the second dance phrase of the *brek* motive, the dancer performs the *gerak asas* in a small semicircular path to the right to face in the opposite direction. The same dance phrases are repeated in the third and fourth measures to bring the dancer back to his or her initial place on the dance floor. (See Appendix B.19.)

SIKU KELUANG

The contemporary dance motive that is perhaps closest to *Zapin Melayu* is the *siku keluang* (flying fox's elbow). In this dance motive, the dancer performs movements similar to the *ragam siku keluang* (flying fox's elbow pattern) motive of *Zapin Melayu*. The dancer begins with a 'right-forward diagonal middle' step on the right foot and this is followed by a 'left side middle' step on the left foot. At this point, the dancer faces his or her right. The remaining two counts of the dance phrase involve two side steps on the right foot and the left foot while the dancer is still facing to the right. In the second phrase of the dance motive, the dancer performs the *gerak asas* in a semicircular dance path to the left. These dance phrases are repeated to bring the dancer back to his initial position. (See Appendix B.20.)

UNTA AND ENJUT

The *unta* (camel) and *enjut* (move up and down) dance motives involve the same movement principles but with different body accentuations. The dancer moves in a forward or forward diagonal path by stepping on the right foot on the first count, then stepping 'forward high' on the left foot and lifting the right foot in the first half of the second count. He follows this by stepping 'forward middle' on the right foot and lifting the left foot in the second half of the second count. This technique is repeated throughout the dance phrase. The combination of the 'forward high' and the 'forward middle' steps on alternate feet in the dance phrase produces the up-and-down motion of the body while travelling in a forward path. When the pelvis is allowed to rock back and forth while the dancer performs the up-and-down motion, the pelvic movement imitates the bobbing of the camel's hump. The dance motive is referred to as *unta* (camel). However, if the torso remains immobile, leaving only the legs to bend and straighten while the up-and-down motion is performed, the dance motive is referred to as *enjut* (move up and down). Both motives may be performed over several measures before the dancer returns to the *gerak asas* phrase, moving in a semicircular path to face the opposite direction. (See Appendix B.21.)

ZIG-ZAK

Like *brek*, the term *zig-zak* is derived from an English word. The word 'zigzag' signifies a series of short, sharp angular movements in alternate directions. The path drawn by a dancer when he or she dances the *zig-zak* dance motive is in the form of a zigzag. The dancer begins by stepping the right foot to 'left-backward diagonal middle' behind the supporting left foot on count one of the dance phrase. The left foot then steps to 'left side middle' while the right foot supports the body on count two. When both feet support the body at the end of count two, the right foot moves to 'left-forward diagonal middle' in front of the supporting left leg on count three. On count four, the left leg moves to the left side of the body with the foot touching the ground while the right foot supports the body. The same dance phrase is then reversed to the right, beginning with the left foot stepping to 'right-backward diagonal middle' behind the supporting right leg. (See Appendix B.22.) Several measures of the *zig-zak* dance phrase may be performed for a single *zig-zak* dance motive.

HALANG

Halang means obstruction in Malay. The *halang* dance motive consists of several phrases of leg movements which teasingly obstruct the dance path of the dance partner. This is done through a series of 'forward diagonal' steps. The dancers begin by stepping to 'right-forward diagonal middle' with the right foot on the first count. This is followed by the left foot stepping to 'left-forward diagonal middle' on the second count. The right foot then resumes the 'right-forward diagonal middle' step on the third count. At the end of the fourth count of the dance phrase, the dancer lifts the left foot while the stationary right leg supports the body. In the second dance phrase of the *halang* motive, the dancer performs the *gerak asas* in a small semicircular path to his or her left to face the opposite direction. (See Appendix B.23.) When two dancers perform the *halang* dance motive opposite one another, they seem, with their 'forward diagonal' steps, to obstruct each other while moving in a straight path.

TEPUK SILAT

The *tepuk silat* dance motive involves hand clapping and thigh slapping on the third and fourth counts of the dance phrase. These actions are performed while the dancer's feet are both planted on the ground with the knees slightly bent in the position of the *silat* martial art. Hence, the name *tepuk silat* is derived from the last two movements of the dance phrase. The first two counts of the dance phrase consist of two regular forward steps as in the *gerak asas*. On the third count of the dance phrase, the dancer steps to 'right side middle' with the right foot, with the left foot supporting the body; at the same time he is clapping with both hands. On the fourth count of the dance phrase, the dancer stands in 'place low' with both feet slightly apart. The fourth count of the dance phrase is punctuated by thigh slapping, with both hands slapping the corresponding thighs. The dancer returns to the *gerak asas* dance phrase, moving in a semicircular path to the left in the second dance phrase. After this, the dancer repeats both dance phrases to complete the *tepuk silat* dance motive before returning to the initial position on the dance floor. (See Appendix B.24.)

WAINAB

The *wainab* dance motive in contemporary *zapin* is simpler and more sedate than that in *Zapin Melayu*. The dancer begins the *wainab* by stepping to 'forward middle' with the right foot on the first count. On the second count of the dance phrase, the dancer lifts the left leg while supporting the body on the right leg. The dancer steps with the left foot to 'forward middle' on the third count and lifts the right leg on the fourth count while supporting the body on the left leg. On the first count of the second dance phrase, the dancer steps to 'forward middle' on the right foot. The left foot is lifted on the second count of the second dance phrase while the right leg supports the body. Throughout all these movements, both hands are placed behind the back. On the third count, the left foot steps to 'forward middle'. The right leg moves behind the left foot and the dancer descends into a crouching position on the fourth count. At this point, the dancer brings both hands to rest on the left thigh. The *wainab* dance motive is repeated as long as the *wainab* music is playing. (See Appendix B.25.)

1. The word *taksim* is derived from *taqsim*, the term for a solo improvisatory instrumental piece in the classical music of the Near East. *Taqsim* as a piece of virtuosity without rhythm was introduced into *nauba* or Arabian suites by Turkish influence in the sixteenth century and into Egypt in the nineteenth century. It is in a free rhythm and may precede the sections of a longer piece of music. *Taqsim* is one of the most favoured instrumental forms in the Near East and may have come into Malay usage with the introduction of the *gambus* or *'ud*. Additional information on the Near Eastern *taqsim* can be obtained from Henry George Farmer, 'The Music of Islam', in *New Oxford History of Music* (London: Oxford University Press, 1957), Vol. 1, pp. 421–77; Josef M. Pacholczyk, 'Secular Classical Music in the Arabian Near East', in Elizabeth May (ed.), *Music of Many Cultures: An Introduction* (Berkeley: University of California Press, 1983), pp. 253–68; and *Grove's Dictionary of Music and Musicians* (London: Macmillan, 1954), Vol. 1, p. 33.

2. Ahmad Fadzil is the leading musician in the National Dance Troupe of Malaysia, the official dance group of the Ministry of Culture, Art and Tourism, Malaysia. He was originally from Muar, Johore, and is known to have acquired the techniques of *gambus* playing from another *gambus* master, Ahmad Yusoh, who plays with the renowned Sri Maharani Ghazal group of Muar. Ahmad Fadzil and Ahmad Yusoh are the most accomplished *gambus* players in Malaysia today.

3. All movement descriptions henceforth will use the dance notation terminologies of Labanotation. (See Ann Hutchinson, *Labanotation or Kinetography Laban: The System of Analyzing and Recording Movements*, New York: Theatre Arts Books, 1977.)

Glossary of Dance Terms

Direction Symbols
The directions in space emanate from a central point recognized as the spatial 'centre'. This point is called 'place', and is represented by the basic symbol of a rectangle. Modifications to the shape of the basic rectangle sign indicate the direction in space.

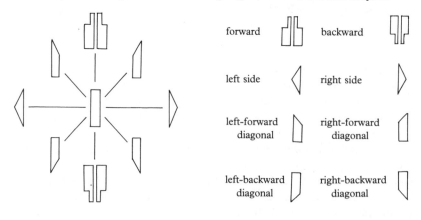

Indication of Level

The level of movement—upward, downward, or horizontal—is indicated by the shading of the directional symbol. A movement in any direction can be horizontal, low, or high in level.

Straight up is 'place high'

Straight down is 'place low'   ▢•

The horizontal middle at
centre place is 'place middle'   ■

4. Maulana is an Arabic term widely used in South-East Asia as a title bestowed upon someone who is regarded as a pious person and who is also a leader of the community. The term Maulana literally means 'Our Lord'. (R. J. Wilkinson, *A Malay–English Dictionary: Part 1 (Alif to Za)*, Singapore: Kelly & Walsh, 1959, p. 664.)

5. Ibid., p. 431. *Sikah* is probably a variation of the word *sekah*. *Sekah* is used to describe the nimbleness of body movements or the agility of a dancer.

6. All the song titles are in Malay except those annotated (Ar.), which indicates an Arabic-derived word.

7. The major recording companies in Malaysia today are WEA Records (a Warner Communications company)—which is also known as Warner Bros Records—CBS Records (Malaysia) Sdn Bhd, EMI (Malaysia) Sdn Bhd, Polygram Records Sdn Bhd, Happy Records Sdn Bhd, and Life Records.

8. Throughout the Malay world, the *gambus* improvisational solo is known as *taksim* and the coda for the *zapin* piece is referred to as *tahtim*. However, in some parts of Johore the term *taksim* may be replaced with the term *tahtim* and the coda for the *zapin* piece may be referred to as *wainab*.

9. The meaning of the term *wainab* is unknown. Many older *zapin* performers in Johore speculated that it may have been a pidgin version of the English word 'wind up', as in winding up a song. Although this argument is of questionable authenticity, it is nevertheless worthy of note.

10. *Silat*, the Malay art of self-defence, is often used in Malay dances as an important source of dance choreography and movement innovations. The dance movements which use the *silat* motives normally display the demonstrative elements of *silat* instead of the combative elements. Hand strikes, kicks, and grappling are the elements used during *silat* demonstrations. When these movements are executed with weapons and become combat-oriented, *silat* becomes a deadly art of self-defence. (Mohd Anis Md Nor, *Randai Dance of Minangkabau Sumatera with Labanotation Scores*, Kuala Lumpur: University of Malaya Press, 1986, pp. 2, 17, and 45.)

7
Zapin in Malaysia: The Contemporary Context

The Taman Budaya and the Institutional Context

THE Taman Budaya (Cultural Garden) was established in June 1966, within the Ministry of Culture, Youth and Sports of Malaysia,[1] to train dancers and musicians in the Malay performance traditions. It was set up at the suggestion of the first Prime Minister of Malaysia, Tunku Abdul Rahman Putra al-Haj, who felt that Malaysia needed a cultural institution that would be directly supervised and supported by the Federal government. The·Tunku envisaged that the Taman Budaya would play a major role in promoting Malay performance traditions among the people of Malaysia and in formulating national performance standards. This ambitious programme began with quite modest accomplishments.

The first task of the Taman Budaya was to recruit dancers, musicians, and dance instructors who would learn and perform a medley of traditional performance repertoires representative of both the national and the regional performance traditions from the various states in the Federation. Inspired by the Bayanihan Philippine Dance Company,[2] the Taman Budaya performers were trained to perform the regional dances and music of Malaysia through the theatrical adaptation of selected genres. The dance choreographers were required to capture the essence of the dance without distorting the original form.[3]

The first group of dance instructors employed by the Taman Budaya were Syed Manaf, Daud Omar, Md Ali, Mak Minah Yem, Mak Raunah, and Ahmad Omar.[4] Mak Minah Yem and Mak Raunah were former *bangsawan* dancers and choreographers who were already familiar with all the Malay dances in the *bangsawan* theatre. It was through their efforts that the dance styles from the *bangsawan* theatre were perpetuated in the Taman Budaya. They taught the dancers of the Taman Budaya dances from the *inang*, *joget*, *asli*, and *zapin* genres as well as new styles created by adapting the choreography of the traditional dances.

Apart from Mak Minah Yem and Mak Raunah, none of the dance instructors in the Taman Budaya had had any formal training in Malay dances. Some had had informal training in one or two dance traditions through their acquaintance with dancers or other performers. However, their interest in promoting and teaching Malay dances enabled them to innovate and experiment with new choreography. All of them were familiar with the four pan-Malaysian folk dances, the *joget*, *inang*, *asli*, and *zapin* dances, and they produced new dance choreographies by innovations on these dances. Each eventually became known for his ability in a particular aspect of Malay dance choreography. Md Ali was famous for the robustness and high energy of his dance choreography. Daud Omar excelled in highly stylized and emotionally expressive dance gestures. He explored the elements of *rasa* (feeling, emotion, or sentiment)[5] in creating new dance motives and styles. Ahmad Omar was skilled at reproducing the *joget gamelan* dances of Trengganu.

Syed Manaf was known for his capability in training beginners in the art of Malay dancing and was the first dance instructor in the country to introduce formal structured classes for the teaching of Malay folk dances. Syed Manaf also developed a formal classification of *zapin* dance motives. He was familiar with the different styles of *zapin* dances that were performed in the urban entertainment parks, the cabarets, and the Malay movie studios in Singapore in the 1950s, having formerly played the drums on the 'trap set' in the dance halls and cabarets. He knew Normadiah, Shaw Brothers' dance instructor and choreographer and was familiar with her dance choreography. He was also a friend of the late P. Ramlee, the actor–director of Malay movies whose interest in Malay folk dances contributed to the creation of new dance motives in the *zapin* dance. Syed Manaf had had a broad exposure to Malay folk dances, including the *zapin* dance, since the 1950s, and this experience proved invaluable in his teaching. He continued the performance style of Malay folk dancing of the 1950s into the 1960s at the Taman Budaya. He was also appointed dance instructor at the Pertak National Youth Training Centre in Selangor.[6]

In the 1970s, the Taman Budaya was expanded and renamed the Komplek Budaya Negara (the National Cultural Complex).[7] Like the Taman Budaya before it, the Komplek Budaya Negara employs a cultural group comprising more than one hundred musicians and dancers.[8]

The establishment of the Taman Budaya and the Komplek Budaya Negara brought the promotion of Malay traditional performances under the aegis of a national cultural institution fully supported by the Malaysian government. Improvements were made in terms of staff recruitment and the teaching of traditional performances. The contemporary *zapin* dance tradition, like the other Malay performance traditions,. became part of the broad curriculum of dance repertoires taught at the Komplek. The teaching and promotion of the dance were regulated by the teaching staff and dance choreographers of the Komplek. They strove for higher standards in *zapin* dancing through better performance quality and consistency of dance techniques from both the resident dancers and the members of the public who attended the periodic dance courses organized by the Ministry of Culture, Youth and Sports. Although the decision to standardize *zapin* dancing was arbitrary, it promoted a search for excellence in the Malay traditional performances, and the standardization was based on a consensus of ideas among the dance instructors and choreographers. Individual dance motives were standardized and became part of the version of *zapin* promoted by the Komplek. This version was disseminated further with the introduction of short-term dance courses for youth organizations and school teachers at the Pertak National Youth Training Centre in Selangor and at the Komplek Budaya Negara itself in Kuala Lumpur. Similar dance training was also provided for dance instructors from the various states. By the middle of the 1970s, Malay folk dances, including *zapin*, were performed all over the country in accordance with the standards set by the Komplek.

By the 1980s, it was clear to all dance practitioners in Malaysia that the Komplek Budaya Negara, in spite of its infrastructural shortcomings,[9] was the only cultural institution in the country that could set the standard for *zapin* dance choreography. Dancers all over the country eagerly copied the *zapin* dance motives and performance styles of the Komplek in order to conform to the national standard.

The role of the Komplek Budaya Negara as guardian of the national culture became more assertive when dance instructors from the institution were invited to teach Malay traditional performances to members of cultural clubs and performance groups in schools, colleges, and universities all over the country. The pan-Malaysian folk dances—*joget, inang, asli,* and *zapin*—were the dance traditions most commonly taught to these students and the *zapin* dance from the repertoire of the Komplek was the one most often taught.

The performers of the Komplek Budaya Negara continue in the role they have held since the 1960s as the national performance group, representing Malaysia in cultural presentations overseas, performing at home for visiting foreign dignitaries and guests of the state, and appearing in specially commissioned performances or theatre productions.

The Contemporary Repertoire

The difference in movement styles between contemporary *zapin* and *Zapin Melayu* can be attributed to the openness with which dancers and choreographers have adapted dance styles from numerous dance repertoires. The current repertoire of dance motives in *zapin* was formulated and introduced by such people as P. Ramlee, Normadiah, Minah Yem, Minah B, Ainon Chik, and Zaharah Agus whose ideas were derived from the Malay movie industry and the *bangsawan* theatre from the 1930s to the early 1960s. The same desire to promote *zapin* as a popular folk tradition was continued by a new generation of choreographers who were first brought to Kuala Lumpur when the Taman Budaya was set up in the early 1960s. These choreographers generally came from a non-theatrical background but they had some knowledge of Malay traditional dances. Their interest in promoting and teaching Malay dances lay not in supplementing dance items in the Malay movies or the *bangsawan* theatre, but in establishing a professional dance troupe with a professional dance repertoire to be a national performance group, capable of representing the nation abroad as cultural ambassadors.

The bringing together of dance instructors and professionally trained dance performers at the Komplek Budaya Negara encouraged creativity and experimentation, keeping the *zapin* dance tradition in a state of continuing evolution. Just as the public had imitated the *zapin* dance motives that had come from the Malay movies, the dance halls in the urban entertainment parks, and the *bangsawan* theatre in the period from the 1930s to the early 1960s, they now imitated new motives introduced by the performers of the Komplek. The phenomenon of the public imitating dance styles from popular institutions has remained an integral part of dance creativity in the *zapin* tradition.

There must have been other factors that have contributed to the creative process whereby the dance has evolved into its contemporary form. The conventional interpretation of tradition in the contemporary *zapin* dance is that the dance focuses on movements of the leg rather than of any other part of the anatomy. No other part of the body should overshadow the importance of the feet in a *zapin* performance. Hand, head, and torso movements are supplementary to the intricacies of the leg movements. However, not all forms of leg movement are allowed in *zapin*. Only leg movements which are fundamentally earthbound, relatively narrow in stride, and seemingly light in step—with an absence of foot stamping—are construed to be proper for *zapin*. The loudness of sound belongs to the drums and should not come from the dancers' feet.

The overwhelming emphasis on leg movements and the primacy of 4/4 time have been crucial factors in the formation of a new repertoire of *zapin* dance motives since the 1930s. Foreign dance traditions that emphasized leg movements were popular with patrons of dance halls and cabarets in those early years. Since the 1980s, attempts have been made to include leg movements borrowed or adapted from Indian dances which are commonly performed by Malaysians of Indian descent. They include dance steps adapted from the *nritta*[10] or pure dance of the Indian classical dance, *Bharata Natyam*[11] and other South Indian folk dance traditions. It is feasible to include adaptations of the leg movements from Indian dances in the *zapin* as long as these movements do not diminish the general characteristics of the latter. The use of Indian dances in new *zapin* dance choreography is, however, less pronounced in Malaysia than in the city of Medan in North Sumatra. The dance groups from the Universitas Sumatera Utara (University of North Sumatra) and the Kutab Ujana Geri, a private institution for the Malay performing arts located in Tanjung Morawa near Medan, have included in their *zapin* dance repertoires dance steps borrowed from the *nritta* of the *Bharata Natyam*.[12] This may perhaps be a pointer indicating the direction in which *zapin* dance choreography is moving.

Many of the dance motives of the *zapin* performed today are a result of the intense adaptation of other dance traditions during the heyday of the Malay movie industry, the *bangsawan* theatre, and the dance halls and cabarets in the urban entertainment parks. The *brek, unta, zig-zak,* and *halang* dance motives can be attributed directly to the influence of popular Latin dance traditions. All the foreign dance traditions that were the sources of new *zapin* dance repertoires shared common elements in performance style with the *zapin* dance. These elements included: the primary influence of 4/4 time in each measure of the dance phrase, the regular four-beat dance count in each dance phrase, and the relatively heavy emphasis on footwork.

Another important aspect of change in the *zapin* tradition was the introduction of women as *zapin* dancers. For traditional *Zapin Melayu* performers, the very idea of allowing women to participate directly as performers was abhorrent. But the new form of popular *zapin* which emerged from the influence of the Malay movies, the *bangsawan* theatre, and the *pentas joget* of the 1950s considered women dance partners as the natural choice for paired dancing. Since there was no segregation of men and women in the dance halls, cabarets, or *pentas joget,* nor in the depiction of dance repertoires in the Malay movies, it became natural for the new *zapin* to include both sexes.

Likewise, the elements of social dancing in the commercial dance halls and the *pentas joget,* such as teasing, cajoling, and flirtatious dance movements, became stylized in *zapin.* However, the prohibition of any form of physical contact between men and women in dancing the *zapin* meant that, in the creation of new dance motives, the idea of teasing and flirting became very subtle and refined. It became the normal practice to keep partners several steps away from each other and to bring them close together, but still never touching. Dance motives such as the *halang, brek,* and all *langkah* and *pusing* dance motives, when performed with the utmost precision, reveal the subtleties of the stylized flirtatious dance movements.

Since the 1970s, and despite the standardization of *zapin,* there have been changes in the repertoires, in terms of improvisations on dance motives and the creation of new dance styles.

Although choreographers and dance instructors have created many new dance motives, some adapted from other performance traditions, the repertoires are constantly under the scrutiny of the performers, and many of the new motives are dropped. Relatively few survive to become part of the standard repertoire. One motive from another performance tradition that has become a permanent element in today's *zapin* performance is the *silat* motive. In the 1970s *silat* movements—sweeping hand motions, flexing of the fingers, and *demi-plié*—were introduced as part of the larger repertoire of the *zapin* dance.[13] Several variations of the *silat* motives were introduced in *zapin,* but most of them disappeared after a short while. The *tepuk silat* dance motive is one *silat* motive that has survived.

With regard to new dance styles, the boldest of all the new *zapin* choreographies to have been created was the *Zapin Hanuman,* named after the monkey-like dance gestures of the monkey god-king of the *Ramayana* epic. This was choreographed in the early 1970s. The music is faster than the regular *zapin* pieces and the monkey-like movements are equally fast and energetic. *Zapin Hanuman* was regarded as highly sensational at the time of its creation because it defied all the preconceived ideas of what a *zapin* dance should be. The almost crouching position of dancers in a prancing-like motive was considered profoundly creative by the younger generation of dancers, but was abhorred by the purists. The bitter-sweet success of *Zapin Hanuman* waned in the early 1980s. This dance is still performed today by some groups in Kuala Lumpur but it has lost much of its popularity. One reason for its decline was the absence of creative innovations in the dance. It remained in the form in which it was first created and was never touched by innovations.

The move towards experimentation and creative choreography has continued among folk dance groups all over the country. With new performance styles and dance motives, folk dance groups hope to perform better than other groups in *zapin* dance choreography competitions. Most of the dance choreographers are aware of the possibility of over-experimentation and the danger of departing from the tradition of *zapin* performances. They prefer to keep their choreography and new dance movements close to the contemporary standards of *zapin*. Innovations are made on the dance steps rather than on the dancers' strides.

The Contemporary Interpretation

The contemporary *zapin* dance is, to some extent, a choreographed folk dance. It requires a certain number of prearranged sets of dance motives and movement phrases which are performed repeatedly in a cycle or in symmetrical alternations. The dance is performed for an audience rather than for impromptu public participation. The convention of sophisticated utilization of floor space and dance motives in contemporary *zapin* challenges dance choreographers and dancers alike to improve their performances with better innovations in their dance choreography. The constant demand for something new or exciting has made performing the contemporary tradition an exhilarating experience for the dancers. This does not, however, allow choreographers and performers to break away from the finesse (*halus*) of *zapin* dancing which had been the hallmark of *Zapin Melayu* in the villages of Johore and in the palaces of the former Malay Sultans in Riau, Siak, Serdang, and Deli in Sumatra. *Zapin* must be performed within the bounds of propriety as defined in Malay culture. Today, performers of *zapin* are still required to dance with much grace and elegance while sustaining the precision of movements and gestures. Leg movements remain the focus of contemporary *zapin* and other bodily movements are supplementary to the intricacies of the leg movements; the notion of an earthbound dance tradition prevails. The light steps must be accompanied by quite narrow strides. Leaps and high skips that would flip the sarongs of female dancers and expose their legs are avoided in order to prevent potentially embarrassing situations.

Not only is contemporary *zapin* construed as a choreographed dance tradition by most Malaysians, it is also considered a dignified dance tradition. In contrast to the glittering era of the *bangsawan* and cabarets in the 1930s, and the glorious years of the Malay movies in the 1950s and 1960s, *zapin* today, in the early 1990s, is associated with the fine artistry of Malay–Arab syncretic culture. *Zapin* is highly regarded as the last bastion of an Arab-derived dance tradition that has contributed to the enrichment of Malay performance traditions. However, it is ironic that it is contemporary *zapin* rather than *Zapin Melayu* (which is closer to Arab traditions) that is accorded this recognition.

Contemporary *zapin* is also esteemed as a manifestation of Islamic influence on indigenous culture. The avoidance of body contact in the dance, the absence of overtly sensuous gestures, and the highly repetitive and symmetrical nature of the dance sequences conform to the abstract quality of Islamic art. The structural characteristic of stylized dance gestures and the symmetrical repetition of dance motives within a pre-scribed floor plan invoke the visual artistic elaboration of a never-ending, arabesque pattern. Lois Lamyā' al-Fārūqī explained arabesques in Islamic visual art as being of two types: the conjunct (*muttasil*, to con-nect) and the disjunct (*munfansil*, to divide into sections). A conjunct arabesque resembles a continuum of abstract motives which are com-bined in an unlimited, never-ending succession. The disjunct or *munfansil* comprises a combination of self-contained motives. Each *zapin* dance motive is analogous to the self-contained units of the *munfansil* arabesque. A *zapin* dance motive is interwoven with other dance motives to produce a larger pattern. The overall arabesque pattern of the *zapin* dance is a result of the continuum of all the dance motives performed in succession. The symmetrical repetition of the *zapin* dance motives combines the elements of the *munfansil* and the *muttasil* of the arabesque pattern of Islamic visual art. The Malays consider the contemporary *zapin* dance an example *par excellence* of Islamic art.[14]

To crown it all, the government of Malaysia has appropriated *zapin* as one of the national folk dance traditions which satisfy the concept of the Malaysian national culture. The concept of a national culture was formulated in 1971 following the race riots of 1969[15] to create a sense of national identity and to bind and integrate the population. The National Culture Policy[16] is based on three main principles:

1. The base of the National Culture is the indigenous culture which is native to the region of the Malay Archipelago.
2. Traits from other cultures, which are pertinent, should be absorbed to enrich the National Culture.
3. Islam and its values play an important role in the formulation of a National Culture.[17]

Although affirmative results of the implementation of the Policy have yet to be seen,[18] the Malaysian government is eager to pursue the Policy.

The *zapin* dance tradition fulfils all three principles of the Malaysian National Culture Policy. First, *zapin* is a dance tradition indigenous to the peoples of the Malay Archipelago, the Malay world or *alam Melayu*. Second, *zapin* was created from the syncretic processes of Malay–Arab culture. Third, *zapin* manifests the arabesque form of Islamic visual art. Thus, *zapin* has become a part of the embodiment of the cultural manifesto of the National Culture Policy of Malaysia.

The Massive Dance Performances

One of the commonest ways of bringing about innovations in the *zapin* dance is through large group performances held in conjunction with a sports event, a commemorative-day celebration, or special festivities. It involves a large group of dancers who are usually recruited from secondary school students in the areas close to the venue of the performance. The students, of whom there may be hundreds, are divided into several smaller groups of about twenty to thirty dancers. Each group of dancers is taught the *gerak asas* or basic dance phrases and the *zapin* dance motives by an instructor. The floor plans and dance motives for each dance group are predetermined by the dance choreographer. The choreographer's first task is to teach all the motives and the floor plan to a group of instructors. The choreographer then has to oversee the training by visiting each group during their practice sessions and checking the work of the instructors. The groups train separately for several weeks before being brought together for practice in a large open area such as a school athletic field or a stadium. This is normally the most challenging time for the choreographer and the instructors because they have to ensure a smooth transition from small group dancing to a massive dance performance. The putting together of the numerous groups into a single body of dancers can be likened to putting together the pieces of a jigsaw puzzle in an open field.

These massive dance performances in large ground formations are opportunities for the dance choreographer to create new dance styles and dance motives. The dance styles and motives choreographed for an open field are not, however, appropriate for the close, picture-framed, proscenium stages. Dance movements are free from the conventions of the *zapin* dance motives. Wider arm sways and broader stepping motions are incorporated in order to enable the dancers to move in unison and in harmony with the large ground formations. To accentuate the dance formations, the *zapin* dancers are often required to perform with dance paraphernalia such as fans, scarves, and hats of various colours. The juxtaposition of colours from the dancers' attire while they perform the *zapin* according to prescribed floor plans in large ground formations is considered a great feat of visual display.

The *zapin* songs such as 'Lancang Kuning' and 'Yaladan', which, in the early 1990s, are popular for large *zapin* group performances, are performed live by a brass band instead of the traditional instruments. Nevertheless, when a brass band is unavailable or is considered too loud, commercially recorded *zapin* songs are played to accompany the dancers in the field.

The use of *zapin* as a medium for massive group performances is widely encouraged by the State Cultural Departments. The government of Malaysia through the Ministry of Culture, Art and Tourism and the State Cultural Departments is keen to promote Malaysian folk dances and music traditions through large-scale performances. The training of school children in massive dance performances is considered to be directly beneficial to the students. It also helps to inculcate the notion of a national culture and a national dance tradition among young Malaysians.

Zapin Rediscovers Its Roots

Malaysian *zapin* dance choreographers have, like those in Sumatra and, to a certain extent, Singapore in the early 1990s, attempted to innovate by restructuring some of the traditional elements of *Zapin Melayu* into contemporary *zapin* performances. Such attempts include choreographing for all-male performers, reverting to the arabesque floor plans of village *zapin*, and the inclusion of pauses in bodily movements on the first count of each dance phrase. The tendency to innovate on these elements, however, is still limited to a few folk dance groups in Malaysia.[19] Only dance choreographers who know how to perform the older village tradition are able to work on such innovations. Although the number of folk dance groups that are able to perform the new version of village *zapin* is limited by virtue of the small number of knowledgeable dance choreographers, the new version nevertheless may permit a restructuring of the older *zapin* dance tradition into the contemporary dance tradition. A return to earlier traditions could perhaps lead *zapin* in Malaysia in a new direction.

1. The Ministry was renamed the Ministry of Culture, Art and Tourism in October 1990. Initially the Taman Budaya was administered by the Ministry's Department of Culture, which had been set up in December 1965.

2. The Bayanihan Philippine Dance Company began as the Filipiniana Folk Music and Dance Committee of the Philippine Women's University (PWU) in the 1950s. The Committee was set up to undertake research on Philippine music and dance. Its research findings were translated into cultural programmes presented at recitals held at the University. The Bayanihan Philippine Dance Company emerged as South-East Asia's most successful performance company after its world premiere performance at the 1958 International Exposition in Brussels, Belgium. The success of the Bayanihan motivated the first director of the Taman Budaya, Dr Ariff Ahmad, to formulate performances which were lively and colourful in the style of the Bayanihan performances. (Personal interview with Dr Ariff Ahmad, August 1989.)

3. Officers of the Taman Budaya recorded dance performances from the various regions in Malaysia in order to reproduce them at the Taman Budaya. The most successful researcher and collecter of cultural materials was Ismail Bakti. As the assistant to the Director, Ismail Bakti was known for his research on Kelantan music and dance and was instrumental in introducing Kelantan performance traditions to the Taman Budaya. He also helped the choreographers and dancers to reproduce them at the Taman Budaya.

4. Personal interview with Dr Ariff Ahmad, August 1989.

5. His dance choreography consistently displayed dramatic expressions performed in stylized dance gestures. Dancers were trained to portray feelings of love, anger, courage, and surprise in their performances. The elements of *rasa* used in Daud's dance choreography also included some aspects of the eight emotions of the *abinaya* in Indian classical dances. A. L. Basham described the *abinaya* as love, courage, loathing, anger, mirth, terror, pity, and surprise. (A. L. Basham, *The Wonder That Was India*, New York: Grove Press, 1959, pp. 385, 417, and 420.)

6. The Pertak National Youth Training Centre was administered by the Youth Division of the Ministry of Culture, Youth and Sports. The centre provided training in the form of skill and leadership courses for Malaysian youths at a national level. As part of the centre's curriculum, Malay folk dances were also taught to the participants.

7. The Taman Budaya was at this time under the administration of the Arts Education and Extension branch, one of the four branches of the Cultural Division of the Ministry of Culture, Youth and Sports. This branch was also responsible for the Komplek Budaya Negara when it was established.

8. *Information Malaysia: 1986 Year Book*, Kuala Lumpur: Berita Publishing, 1986, p. 265.

9. The buildings of the Komplek Budaya Negara consist of one new building (which replaced an old dilapidated colonial building deemed structurally unsafe) and two wooden double-storey buildings. There are several studios which are used for dance, music, and theatre classes and rehearsals. The basement room of one of the buildings was converted into a music studio. The Komplek awaits the building of a permanent structure that will provide better studio facilities, administrative units, classrooms, and an audio–visual studio.

10. *Nritta* is composed of basic dance units known as *adavu*. Each *adavu* contains three elements, namely *stanaka* (a basic standing position), *chari* (movements of the legs and feet), and *nritta hastas* (decorative hand gestures). Dance steps which are improvised for the experimental *zapin* dance motives are adapted from the *chari* element (movements of the legs and feet) of the *adavus* of the *nritta*.

11. *Bharata Natyam* originated from the State of Tamil Nadu in South India. It is performed as a solo by women. The dance was previously known as *sadir* or *dasi attam* and was performed by the *devadasis* which literally means 'female servant of the deity'. For more information on the *devadasis*, see Frederique Apffel Marglin, *Wives of the God-King: The Rituals of the Devadasis of Puri*, Delhi: Oxford University Press, 1985.

12. The *zapin* dancers in Medan also perform the new *zapin* dance repertoires for a television series on traditional entertainment on TVRI (Television and Radio Indonesia).

13. Daud Omar, a dance choreographer with the Komplek Budaya Negara in the 1970s, introduced numerous *silat* movements in the new *zapin* repertoire. His versions of *zapin budiman* and *makan sireh* are rich in *silat* movements and were choreographed for all-male performances.

14. For more information on the aesthetics of Islamic art, see Lois Lamyā' al-Fārūqī, *Islam and Art*, Islamabad: National Hijra Council, 1985.

15. The race riots of 13 May 1969 brought four days of bloody communal violence to Kuala Lumpur, Penang, and other cities and towns in Peninsular Malaysia. The ethnic disturbances which erupted the day after the Federal elections had resulted from inter-racial animosity on issues pertaining to education and language, amongst others; all of which were fought on a highly emotional level during the election campaign. The aftermath of the race riots brought about a restructuring of the economy and society through the implementation of long-term economic planning. The New Economic Policy, the Bumiputra's (sons of the soil) special privileges, and the National Language Policy were introduced to restructure society and to create national unity.

16. The National Culture Congress (Kongres Kebudayaan Kebangsaan), held in Kuala Lumpur in 1971, drew up the guidelines which became the basis for the National Culture Policy. The Policy is implemented by various government agencies, voluntary bodies, and the general public, as well as by the Ministry of Culture, Art and Tourism.

17. *Information Malaysia: 1986 Year Book*, p. 264.

18. The National Culture Policy has been considered by many people to be too academic in perspective and too idealistic in its goal. The Policy is also widely criticized for being less than action-oriented. In spite of the countless seminars and congresses held to discuss the National Culture, the Policy has lacked constructive implementation. The general feeling among many Malaysians, however, is that the people themselves will decide on the form of the National Culture that will eventually emerge. ('Kebudayaan Kebangsaan setelah 18 Tahun', *Dewan Budaya*, August 1989, pp. 11–16.)

19. There are three groups of dancers which are actively pursuing this trend; one each in Kuala Trengganu, Penang, and Kuala Lumpur.

Appendices

APPENDIX A
The Music Transcriptions

Music Transcriptions for *Zapin* Dance
Special Symbols in the Music Notation

SYMBOL	MEANING
	The original starting pitch.
	Sometimes the note(s) in parentheses is(are) not played.
	A pitch slightly higher than the written note.
	A pitch slightly lower than the written note.
	Upward slide to the written note.
	The pitch is played in steady, even sixteenth notes for the time duration written.
	The pitch is played in steady, even eighth notes for the time duration written.
	In the *Marwas* staves, notes written in the third space are high-timbre (played near the rim of the drum skin). Notes written in the first space are low-timbre (played near the centre of the drum skin).
	High-pitched sound.
	Medium-pitched sound.
	Low-pitched sound.

APPENDIX A.1
Lagu Zapin Maulana

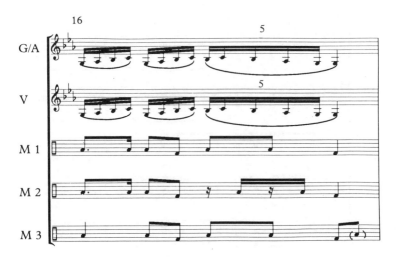

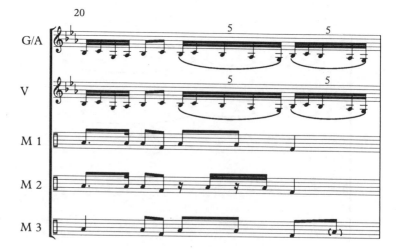

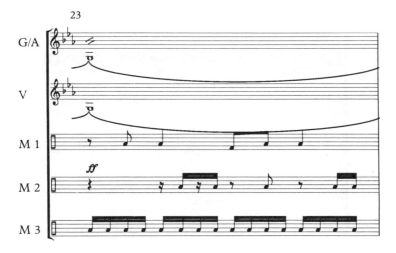

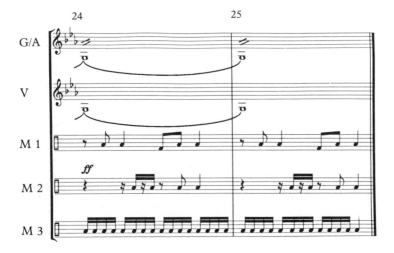

APPENDIX A.2
Lagu Gambus Palembang

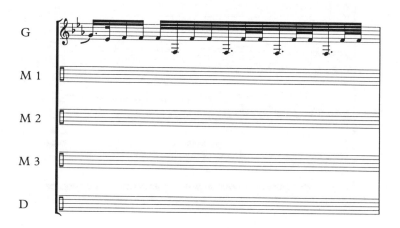

APPENDIX A.3
Lagu Sikah Masri

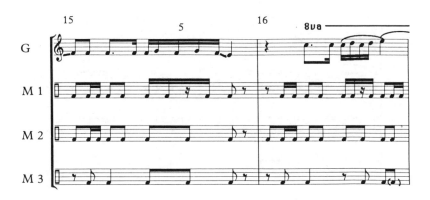

APPENDIX A.4
Lagu Lancang Kuning
(Batu Pahat)

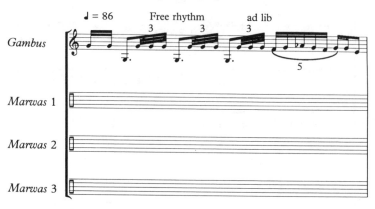

APPENDIX A.5
Lagu Lancang Kuning
(Kuala Lumpur)

APPENDIX B
The Dance Notations

APPENDIX B.1
Gerak Asas of *Zapin Melayu*

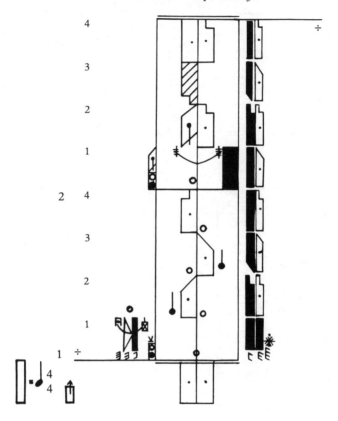

APPENDIX B.2
Gerak Asas of Contemporary *Zapin*

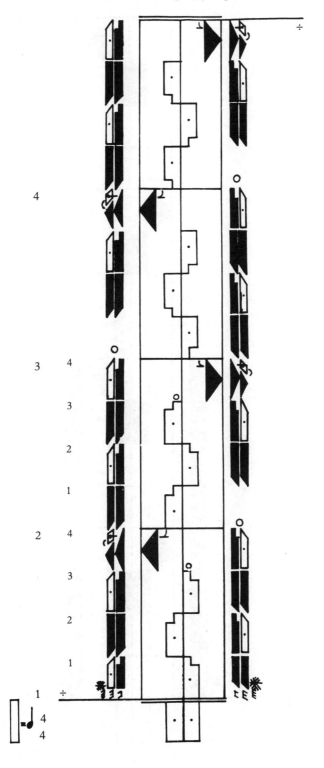

APPENDIX B.3
Gerak Asas of Contemporary *Zapin*: Variation

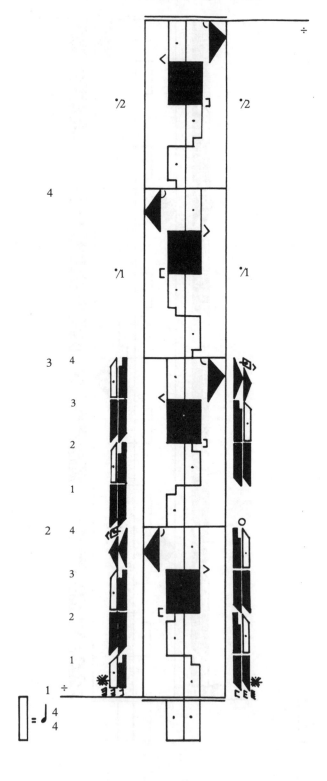

APPENDIX B.4
Sembah Dance Motive

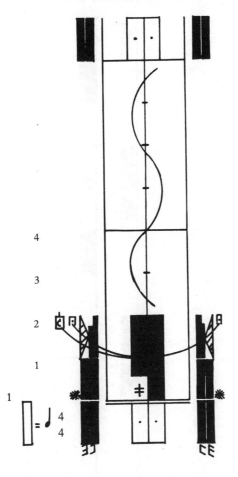

APPENDIX B.5
Sembah Dance Motive

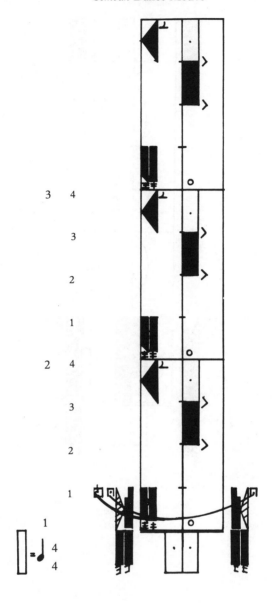

APPENDIX B.6
Sembah Dance Motive

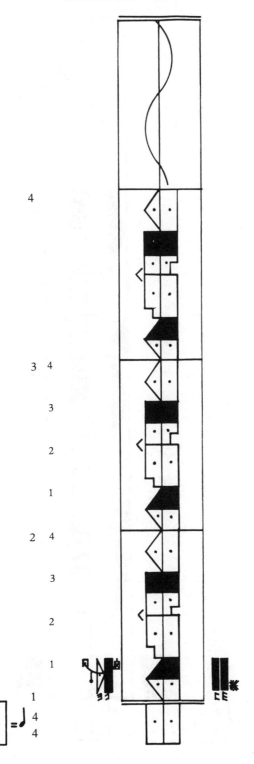

APPENDIX B.7
Ragam Dance Motive

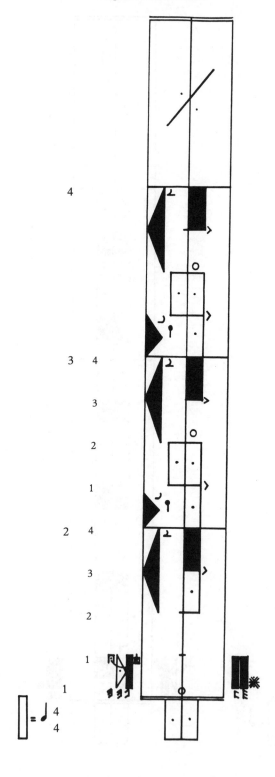

APPENDIX B.8
Ragam Dance Motive

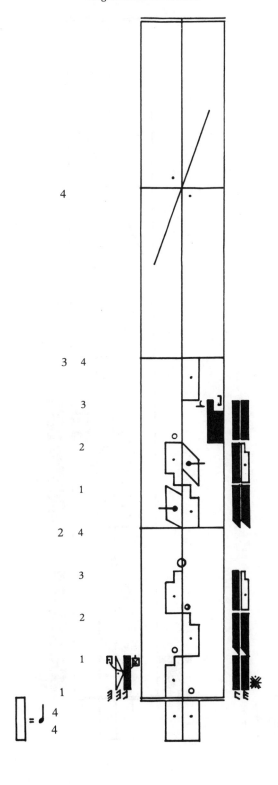

APPENDIX B.9
Ragam Dance Motive

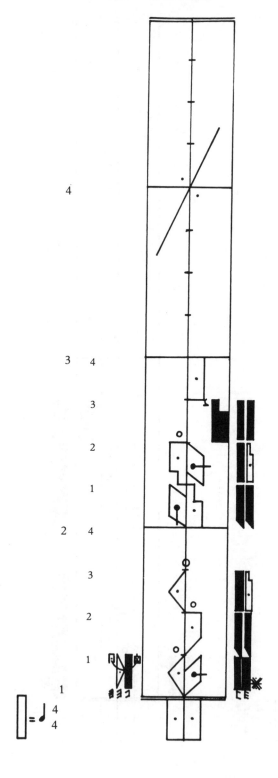

APPENDIX B.10
Ragam Dance Motive

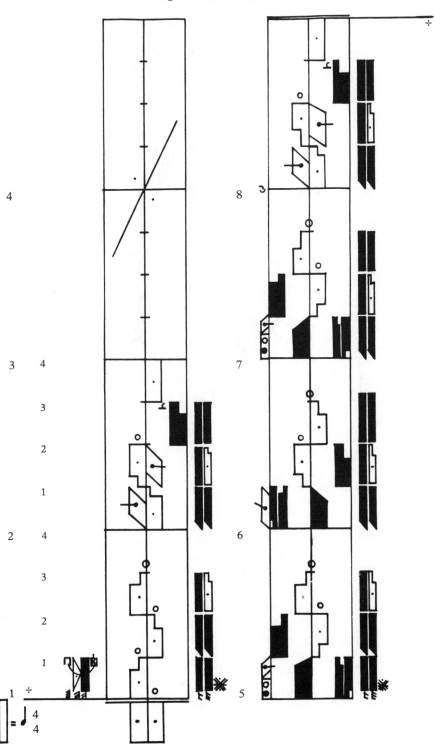

APPENDIX B.11
Anak Ayam Dance Motive

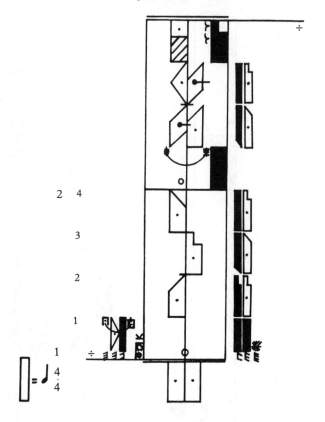

APPENDIX B.12
Anak Ikan Dance Motive

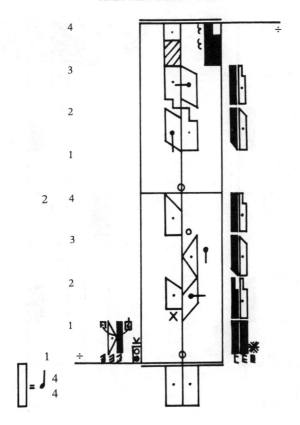

APPENDIX B.13
Lompat Dance Motive

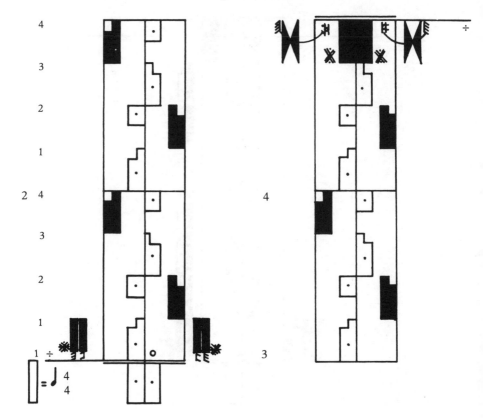

APPENDIX B.14
Pusau Belanak Dance Motive

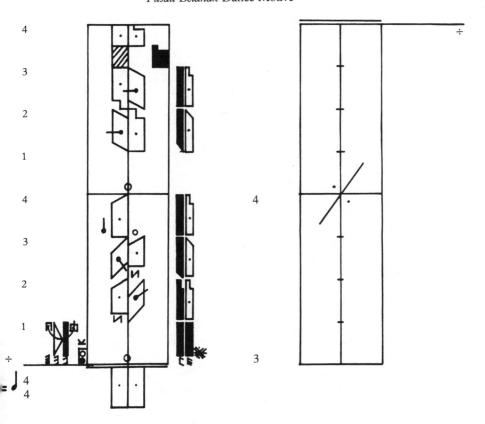

APPENDIX B.15
Pecah Dua Floor Plan

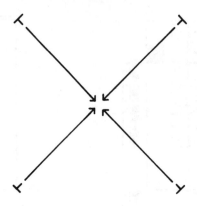

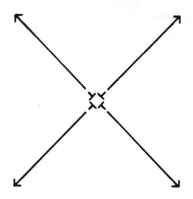

APPENDIX B.16
Sisip Dance Motive

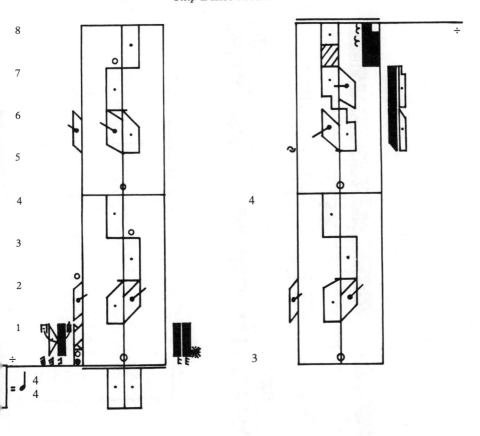

APPENDIX B.17
Langkah Hadapan and *Langkah Belakang*

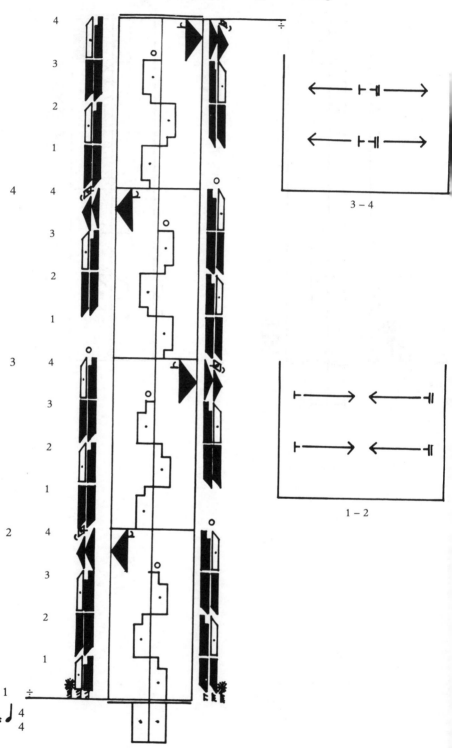

APPENDIX B.18
Pusing Dance Motive

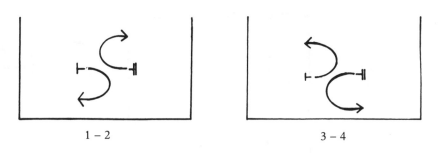

1 – 2   3 – 4

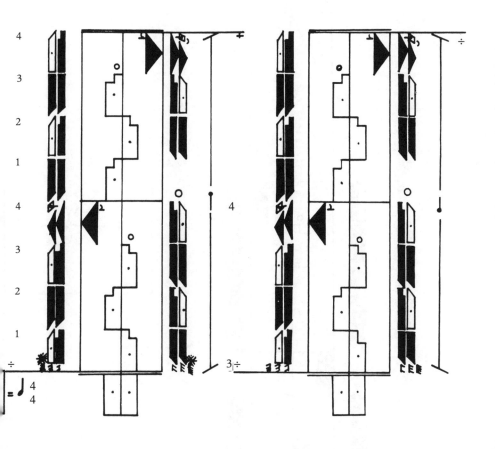

APPENDIX B.19
Brek Dance Motive

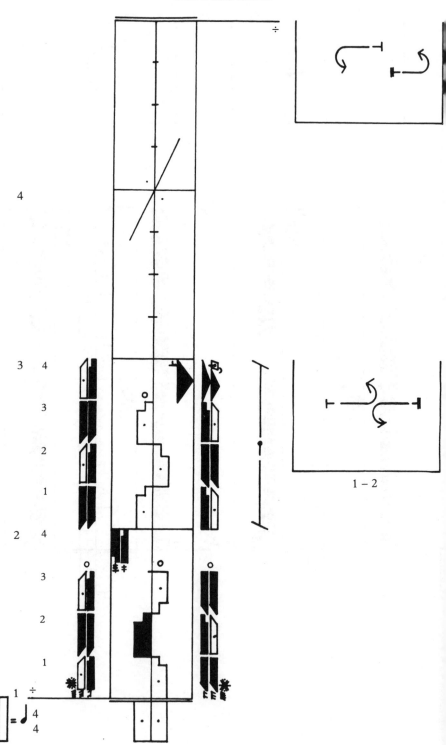

APPENDIX B.20
Siku Keluang Dance Motive

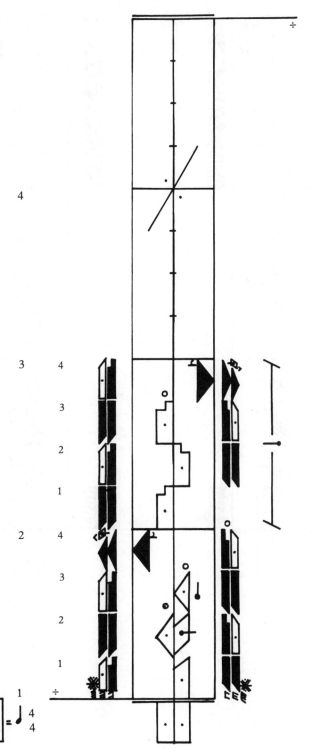

APPENDIX B.21
Unta and *Enjut* Dance Motive

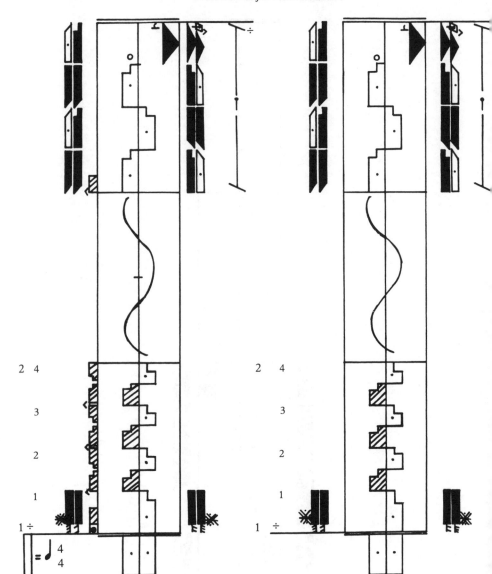

APPENDIX B.22
Zig-zak Dance Motive

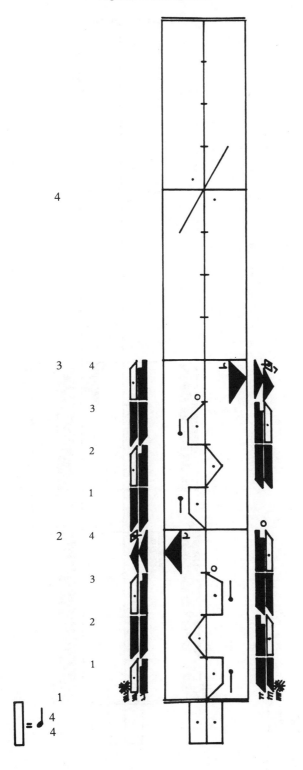

APPENDIX B.23
Halang Dance Motive

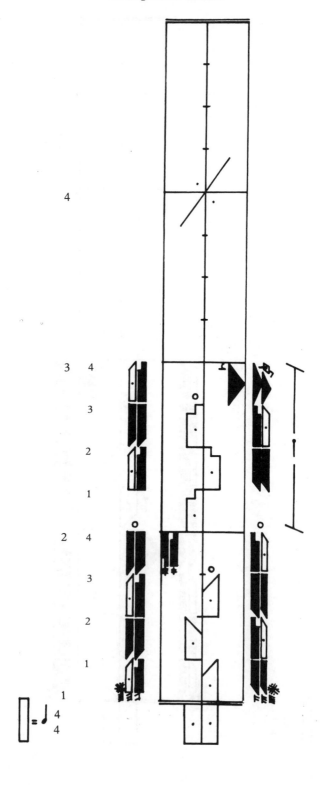

APPENDIX B.24
Tepuk Silat Dance Motive

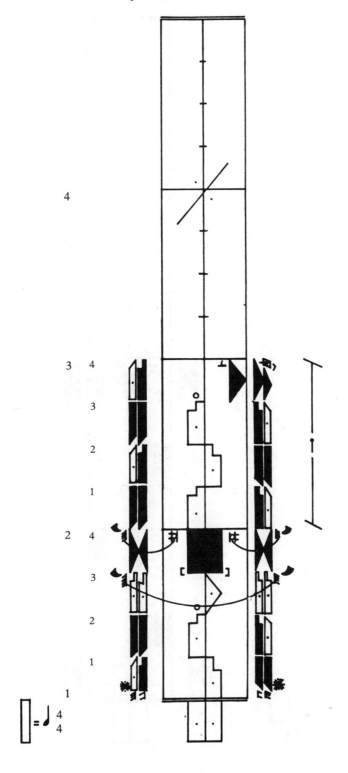

APPENDIX B.25
Wainab Dance Motive

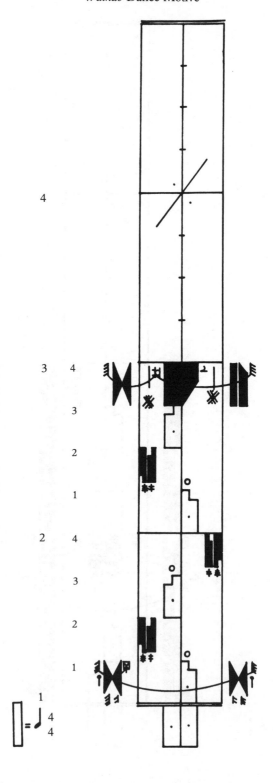

Bibliography

A. Samad Ahmad (ed.), *Kerajaan Johor–Riau* (Kuala Lumpur: Dewan Bahasa dan Pustaka, Kementerian Pelajaran Malaysia, 1985).

Abdul Latiff Abu Bakar (ed.), *Warisan Dunia Melayu: Teras Peradaban Malaysia* (Kuala Lumpur: Biro Penerbitan GAPENA, 1985).

Abi, *Filem Melayu Dahulu dan Sekarang* (Shah Alam: Marwilis Publisher, 1987).

Achmad, Hisyam, *Latar Belakang Sosial Budaya Masyarakat Keturunan Arab di Indonesia* (Bandung: Lembaga Kebudayaan Universitas Padjadjaran, 1976).

Ahmad Fawzi Basri, *Johor 1855–1917: Pentadbiran dan Perkembangannya* (Petaling Jaya: Penerbit Fajar Bakti, 1988).

Alwi bin Sheikh Alhady, *Malay Customs and Traditions* (Singapore: Donald Moore Press, 1967; repr. New York: AMS Press, 1981).

Andaya, Leonard Y., *The Kingdom of Johor 1641–1728* (Kuala Lumpur: Oxford University Press, 1975).

Andaya, Barbara Watson and Andaya, Leonard Y., *A History of Malaysia* (London: Macmillan Education Ltd., 1987).

Ariff Ahmad, *Seni Musik Keroncong* (Kuala Lumpur: Pusat Kebudayaan Universiti Malaya, 1980).

Armstrong, Lucile, *Dances of Portugal* (London: Max Parrish, 1957).

Asmah Haji Omar, *The Malay Peoples of Malaysia and Their Languages* (Kuala Lumpur: Dewan Bahasa dan Pustaka, Kementerian Pelajaran Malaysia, 1983).

Awang Sudjai Hairul and Yusoff Khan (eds.), *Kamus Lengkap* (Petaling Jaya: Pustaka Zaman, 1986).

Baharudin Latif, *Krisis Filem Melayu* (Kuala Lumpur: Insular Pub. House, 1983).

Banks, David J., *Malay Kinship* (Philadelphia: Institute for the study of Human Issues, 1983).

Barnouw, Erik and Krishnaswamy, S., *Indian Film* (New York: Oxford University Press, 1980).

Basham, A. L., *The Wonder That Was India* (New York: Grove Press, 1959).

Bayanihan (Manila: Bayanihan Folk Arts Center, Pearl Diadem Year, 1987).

Becker, Judith, 'Kroncong, Indonesian Popular Music', *Asian Music*, 7 (1), pp. 14–18.

Bilainkin, George, *Hail, Penang!* (London: Sampson Low, Marston & Co., 1932).

'Branle', *Grove's Dictionary of Music and Musicians*, 5th edn. (London: Macmillan, 1954).

'Branle', *Harvard Dictionary of Music*, 2nd edn. (Cambridge, Massachusetts: the Belknap Press of Harvard University Press, 1969).

Chopyak, James D., 'Music in Modern Malaysia: A Survey of the Musics

Affecting the Development of Malaysian Popular Music', *Asian Music*, 18 (1), pp. 111–38.

Daillie, Francois-Rene, *Alam Pantun Melayu: Studies on the Malay Pantun* (Kuala Lumpur: Dewan Bahasa dan Pustaka, Ministry of Education, 1988).

Drewes, G. W. J., 'New Light on the Coming of Islam to Indonesia?' in Ahmad Ibrahim, Sharon Siddique, and Yasmin Hussain (eds.), *Readings on Islam in Southeast Asia* (Singapore: Institute of Southeast Asian Studies, 1985).

Ernst, Heins, 'Kroncong and Tanjidor: Two Cases of Urban Folk Music in Jakarta', *Asian Music*, 7 (1), pp. 20–32.

Farmer, Henry George, 'The Music of Islam', *New Oxford History of Music*, Vol. 1 (London: Oxford University Press, 1957).

Fārūqī, Lois Lamyā' al-, 'Dance as an Expression of Islamic Culture', *Dance Research Journal*, 10 (2) (Spring–Summer, 1978), pp. 6–13.

――, *Islam and Art* (Islamabad: National Hijra Council, 1985).

Geertz, Clifford, *Interpretation of Cultures* (New York: Basic Books, 1973).

Gennep, Arnold van, *The Rites of Passage*, Translated by Monika B. Vizedom and Gabrielle L. Caffee (Chicago: The University of Chicago Press, 1960).

Ghulam Sarwar Yousof, 'Bangsawan: Opera Melayu (Bahagian Pertama)', *Dewan Budaya*, November 1986, pp. 51–4.

――, 'Bangsawan: Opera Melayu (Bahagian Akhir)', *Dewan Budaya*, December 1986, pp. 33–8.

――, 'Bangsawan: The People's Opera', *Pulau Pinang*, January–February 1989.

Grove's Dictionary of Music and Musicians, Vol. 1 (London: Macmillan, 1954).

H. T. S. Umar Muhammad, Tenas Effendy, and T. Razak Jaafar, *Silsilah Keturunan Raja-Raja Kerajaan Siak Sri Indrapura dan Kerajaan Pelalawan* (Pekanbaru, Riau: Bumi Pustaka, 1988).

Hadidjaja, Tardjan, *Adat Raja-Raja Melayu* (Kuala Lumpur: Penerbitan Pustaka Antara, 1964).

Hamidy, UU, *Riau sebagai Pusat Bahasa dan Kebudayaan Melayu* (Pekanbaru, Riau: Bumi Pustaka, 1988).

Hanna, Judith Lynne, *To Dance is Human* (Austin: University of Texas Press, 1980).

――, *The Performer–Audience Connection Emotion to Metaphor in Dance and Society* (Austin: University of Texas Press, 1983).

Harun Mat Piah (ed.), *Gamelan Malaysia* (Kuala Lumpur: Kementerian Kebudayaan, Belia dan Sukan Malaysia, 1983).

Harvard Dictionary of Music, 2nd edn. (Cambridge, Massachusetts: The Belknap Press of Harvard University Press, 1969).

Hutchinson, Ann, *Labanotation or Kinetography Laban: The System of Analyzing and Recording Movements* (New York: Theater Arts Books, 1977).

'India', *The New Encyclopaedia Britannica*, 15th edn., Vol. 21 (Chicago: Encyclopaedia Britannica, 1987).

Indonesian Film Catalogue (Jakarta: National Film Council of Indonesia, 1982).

Information Malaysia: 1986 Year Book (Kuala Lumpur: Berita Publishing, 1986).

Information Malaysia: 1989 Year Book (Kuala Lumpur: Berita Publishing, 1989).

Jamil Sulong, 'Aperçu Sur L'Histoire Du Cinema Malais', *Archipel*, 5 (1973), pp. 231–41.

Jeffrey, Robin, *Asia: The Winning of Independence* (New York: St. Martin's Press, 1981).

Kaeppler, Adrienne L., 'Dance in Anthropological Perspective', *Annual Review of Anthropology*, 7 (1978), pp. 31–49.

———, 'Method and Theory in Analysing Dance Structure with an Analysis of Tongan Dance', *Ethnomusicology*, 16 (1972), pp. 173–217.

Kamus Besar Bahasa Indonesia (Jakarta: Departemen Pendidikan dan Kebudayaan Republik Indonesia, 1988).

'Kebudayaan Kebangsaan setelah 18 Tahun', *Dewan Budaya*, August 1989.

Khadim, Sa'd al-, *Al-Raqs al-Sha'bi fi Misr* (al-Qahirah [Cairo]: Al-Hay'ah al-Misriyah al-'Ammah lil-Kuttab, 1972).

Ku Zam Zam Ku Idris, 'Nobat Diraja Kedah: Warisan Seni Muzik Istana Melayu Melaka', in Abdul Latiff Abu Bakar (ed.), *Warisan Dunia Melayu: Teras Peradaban Malaysia* (Kuala Lumpur: Biro Penerbitan GAPENA, 1985).

Kurath, Gertrude Prokosch, *Half a Century of Dance Research* (Flagstaff, Arizona: Cross Cultural Dance Resources, 1986).

Lane, Edward William, *An Arabic–English Lexicon* (Beirut, Lebanon: Libraire du Liban, 1980).

Lange, Roderyk, *The Nature of Dance: An Anthropological Perspective* (London: Macdonald and Evans, 1975).

Langer, Susanne, *Feeling and Form: A Theory of Art* (London: Routledge & Kegan Paul, 1953).

Laporan Hasil Penyelenggaraan Studi Perbandingan Tari Zapin Se-Daerah Riau (Pekanbaru, Riau: Proyek Pengembangan Kesenian Riau, 1981).

Li, Tania, *Malays in Singapore: Culture, Economy, and Ideology* (Singapore: Oxford University Press, 1989).

Mahayudin Haji Yahaya, 'Latarbelakang Sejarah Keturunan Sayid di Malaysia', in Khoo Kay Kim et al. (eds.), *Tamaddun di Malaysia* (Kuala Lumpur: Persatuan Sejarah Malaysia, 1980).

Maletic, Vera, *Body, Space, Expression: The Development of Rudolf Laban's Movement and Dance Concepts* (Berlin and New York: Mouton de Gruyter, 1987).

Malm, William P., *Music Cultures of the Pacific, the Near East, and Asia* (New Jersey: Prentice Hall, 1967).

Marglin, Frederique Apffel, *Wives of the God-King: The Rituals of the Devadasis of Puri* (Delhi: Oxford University Press, 1985).

Marsden, William, *A Dictionary and Grammar of the Malayan Language* (Singapore: Oxford University Press, 1984).

Martin, Pierre, 'L'Influence Arabe en Malaisie', *L'Afrique et Asie*, 61 (1963), pp. 23–39.

Matheson, Virginia, 'Mahmud, Sultan of Riau and Lingga (1823–1864)', *Indonesia*, 13 (1972), pp. 119–46.

——— (ed.), *Tuhfat al-Nafis: Raja Haji Ahmad dan Raja Ali Haji* (Kuala Lumpur: Penerbit Fajar Bakti, 1982).

Merriam, Alan P., *The Anthropology of Music* (Evanston, Ill.: Northwestern University Press, 1987).

Meulen, D. Van Der, *Aden to the Hadhramaut: A Journey in South Arabia* (London: John Murray, 1947).

Meulen, D. Van Der and Wissmann, H. Von, *Hadramaut: Some of Its Mysteries Unveiled* (Leyden: E. J. Brill, 1964).

Milner, A. C., *Kerajaan: Malay Political Culture on the Eve of Colonial Rule* (Tucson, Arizona: The University of Arizona Press, 1982).

Mohd Anis Md Nor, 'Kreasi Dramatari Dalam Suasana Gamelan Melayu', in

Hashim Awang A. R. (ed.), *Fenomena* (Kuala Lumpur: Jabatan Pengajian Melayu, Universiti Malaya, 1988).

―――, *Randai Dance of Minangkabau Sumatera with Labanotation Scores* (Kuala Lumpur: University of Malaya Press, 1986).

Mohd Aris Haji Othman, *Identiti Etnik Melayu* (Petaling Jaya: Penerbit Fajar Bakti, 1985).

Mohd Taib Osman, *Bunga Rampai Kebudayaan Melayu* (Kuala Lumpur: Dewan Bahasa dan Pustaka, Kementerian Pendidikan Malaysia, 1988).

―――, *Kebudayaan Melayu dalam Beberapa Persoalan* (Kuala Lumpur: Dewan Bahasa dan Pustaka, Kementerian Pendidikan Malaysia, 1988).

――― (ed.), *Malaysian World-View* (Singapore: Institute of Southeast Asian Studies, 1985).

―――, *Masyarakat Melayu: Struktur, Organisasi dan Manifestasi* (Kuala Lumpur: Dewan Bahasa dan Pustaka, Kementerian Pendidikan Malaysia, 1989).

―――, *Traditional Drama and Music of Southeast Asia* (Kuala Lumpur: Dewan Bahasa dan Pustaka, Kementerian Pelajaran Malaysia, 1974).

Mustapha Kamil Yassin, 'The Malay Bangsawan', in Mohd Taib Osman (ed.), *Traditional Drama and Music of Southeast Asia* (Kuala Lumpur: Dewan Bahasa dan Pustaka, Kementerian Pelajaran Malaysia, 1974), pp. 143–53.

Nagata, Judith A., 'What Is a Malay? Situational Selection of Ethnic Identity in a Plural Society', *American Ethnologist*, Vol. 2, No. 2 (1974).

Navis, A. A., *Alam Terkembang Jadi Guru: Adat dan Kebudayaan Minangkabau* (Jakarta: Grafitipers, 1984).

Osborn, Milton, *Southeast Asia: An Illustrated Introductory History* (Boston: George Allen & Unwin, 1983).

Pacholczyk, Josef M., 'Secular Classical Music in the Arabian Near East', in Elizabeth May (ed.), *Music of Many Cultures: An Introduction* (Berkeley: University of California Press, 1983).

Panitia Penyelenggara Studi Perbandingan Tari Zapin Se-Daerah Riau, *Laporan Hasil Penyelenggaraan Studi Perbandingan Tari Zapin Se-Daerah Riau* (Pekanbaru, Riau: Pusat Olah Seni Tari Tangkerang Pekanbaru, Proyek Pengembangan Kesenian Riau, 1981).

Pertemuan Dunia Melayu '82 (Kuala Lumpur: Dewan Bahasa dan Pustaka, Kementerian Pelajaran Malaysia, 1987).

Poerwadarminta, W. J. S. (ed.), *Kamus Umum Bahasa Indonesia* (Jakarta: Dinas Penerbitan Balai Pustaka, 1965).

Raffee, W. G., *Dictionary of the Dance* (New York: A. S. Barnes and Company, 1975).

Rahmah Bujang, *Sejarah Perkembangan Drama Bangsawan di Tanah Melayu dan Singapura* (Kuala Lumpur: Dewan Bahasa dan Pustaka, Kementerian Pelajaran Malaysia, 1975).

Rahman Shaari, *Kualiti Drama dan Filem Melayu* (Kuala Lumpur: Munora, 1983).

Raja Ali Haji Ibn Ahmad, *The Precious Gift: Tuhfat al-Nafis*, An annotated translation by Virginia Matheson and Barbara Watson Andaya (Kuala Lumpur: Oxford University Press, 1982).

Reid, Anthony, *Southeast Asia in the Age of Commerce 1450–1680* (New Haven: Yale University Press, 1988).

Roff, William R., 'The Malayo-Muslim World of Singapore at the Close of the Nineteenth Century', *Journal of Asian Studies*, Vol. XXIV, No. 1 (1964).

Royce, Anya Peterson, *The Anthropology of Dance* (Bloomington: Indiana University Press, 1977).

Sabrin, Amrin (ed.), *Ragam Zapin Daerah Riau* (Pekanbaru, Riau: Bidang Kesenian, Kanwil Depdikbud, n.d.).

Sachs, Curt, *World History of the Dance* (New York: Norton, 1937).

Schechner, Richard, *Between Theater & Anthropology* (Philadelphia: University of Pennsylvania Press, 1987).

Sekilas Perkembangan Tarian Zapin Daerah Riau, Makalah Studi Perbandingan Tari Zapin pada Temu Duta Seni Daerah Tahun 1984/1985, 18–22 October 1984 (Jambi: Departemen Pendidikan dan Kebudayaan Kantor Wilayah Propinsi Riau, 1984).

Sharifah Zinjuaher H. M. Ariffin and Hang Tuah Arshad, *Sejarah Filem Melayu* (Kuala Lumpur: Penerbitan Sri Sharifah, 1980).

Sheets, Maxine, *The Phenomenology of Dance* (Madison: University of Wisconsin Press, 1966).

Sheets, Maxine and Johnstone (eds.), *Illuminating Dance: Philosophical Explorations* (Lewisburg: Bucknell University Press; London: Associated University Press, 1984).

Sheppard, Mubin, *Taman Saujana: Dance, Drama, Music and Magic In Malaya Long and Not-so-Long Ago* (Petaling Jaya: International Book Service, 1983).

Sim, Katherine, *Malayan Landscape* (London: Michael Joseph, 1946).

Singapore 1987 (Singapore: Information Division, Ministry of Communications and Information, 1987).

Spencer, Paul (ed.), *Society and the Dance: The Social Anthropology of Process and Performance* (Cambridge: Cambridge University Press, 1985).

Sulaiman Jeem and Abdul Ghani Hamid, *Mengenang Pak Zubir* (Singapore: Pustaka Melayu Publisher, 1988).

Talib, Yusof A., 'Le Hadramis et Le Monde Malais', *Archipel*, 7 (1974), pp. 41–68.

Tengku Luckman Sinar (ed.), *Sari Sejarah Serdang 1* (Jakarta: Departemen Pendidikan dan Kebudayaan, Proyek Penerbitan Buku Sastra Indonesia dan Daerah, 1986).

———, *Sari Sejarah Serdang 2* (Jakarta: Departemen Pendidikan dan Kebudayaan, Proyek Penerbitan Buku Sastra Indonesia dan Daerah, 1986).

The Bayanihan Experience (Manila: The Bayanihan Folk Arts Center, 1987).

Thomas, Philip L., *Like Tigers Around a Piece of Meat: The Baba Style of Dondang Sayang* (Singapore: Institute of Southeast Asian Studies, 1986).

Tibbetts, G. R., 'Early Muslim Traders in South-East Asia', *Journal of the Malayan Branch of the Royal Asiatic Society*, Vol. XXX, Part I (1957).

Trocki, Carl A., *Prince of Pirates: The Temenggongs and the Development of Johor and Singapore 1784–1885* (Singapore: Singapore University Press, 1979).

Tunku Abdul Rahman, *As a Matter of Interest* (Kuala Lumpur: Heinemann Educational Books (Asia), 1982).

Turner, Victor, *The Anthropology of Performance* (New York: PAJ Publications, 1988).

———, *Dramas, Fields, and Metaphors: Symbolic Action in Human Society* (Ithaca, New York: Cornell University Press, 1987).

———, *The Ritual Process: Structure and Anti-Structure* (Ithaca, New York: Cornell University Press, 1987).

———, *From Ritual to Theater: The Human Seriousness of Play* (New York: PAJ Publications, 1982).

Utz, Peter, 'A Confederacy of Format: Part 1', *Av Video*, April 1989, pp. 54–62.

Vredenbregt, J., 'Bawean Migrations', *BKI* (Bijdragen tot de Taal-, Land- en Volkenkunde), 123 (1964), pp. 267–86.

162   BIBLIOGRAPHY

Wan Abdul Kadir, *Budaya Popular dalam Masyarakat Melayu Bandaran* (Kuala Lumpur: Dewan Bahasa dan Pustaka, Kementerian Pendidikan Malaysia, 1988).

_____, 'Hiburan dalam Masyarakat Melayu Bandaran 1870 hingga 1941: Satu Kajian Tentang Pertumbuhan Budaya Popular', Ph.D. diss., University of Malaya, 1980.

_____, 'Pertumbuhan Budaya Popular Masyarakat Melayu Bandaran sebelum Perang Dunia Kedua', in Mohd Taib Osman and Wan Kadir Yusoff (eds.), *Kajian Budaya dan Masyarakat di Malaysia* (Kuala Lumpur: Dewan Bahasa dan Pustaka, Kementerian Pelajaran Malaysia, 1983), pp. 53–109.

_____, 'Taman Hiburan: Satu Penilaian Sosial', *Purba*, Bil. 2 (1983), pp. 96–102.

Webster's Unabridged Dictionary of the English Language (New York: Portland House, 1989).

Wee, Vivienne, 'Material Dependence and Symbolic Independence: Constructions of Melayu Ethnicity in Island Riau, Indonesia', in Terry A. Rambo, Kathleen Gillogly, and Karl L. Hutterer (eds.), *Ethnic Diversity and the Control of Natural Resources in Southeast Asia* (Ann Arbor, Michigan: Michigan Papers on South and Southeast Asia, 1988).

_____, 'The Malay of Riau: Culture and Ecology in Historical Perspective (A Preliminary Report)', Paper presented to the Persidangan Antarabangsa Pengajian Melayu, Kuala Lumpur, September 1979.

_____, 'Melayu: Hierarchies of Being in Riau', Australian National University, Canberra, 1985.

Wehr, Hans, *A Dictionary of Modern Written Arabic*, ed. J. Milton Cowan (Wiesbaden: Otto Harrassowitz, 1961).

Wilkinson, R. J., *A Malay–English Dictionary (Romanised): Part 1 (A–K)* (London: Macmillan & Co. Ltd., 1959).

_____, *A Malay–English Dictionary: Part 1 (Alif to Za)* (Singapore: Kelly & Walsh, 1901).

Winstedt, Richard Olof, *A History of Johor (1365–1895)*, (Kuala Lumpur: Malaysian Branch of the Royal Asiatic Society, 1979).

_____, *An Unabridged Malay–English Dictionary*, 6th edn. (Kuala Lumpur: Marican, 1965).

Index